Private Investigation

Short Story Confessions of a Private Investigator

(A Pocket-friendly Step by Step Guide)

Bonnie Hayes

Published By **Chris David**

Bonnie Hayes

All Rights Reserved

Private Investigation: Short Story Confessions of a Private Investigator (A Pocket-friendly Step by Step Guide)

ISBN   978-1-77485-870-7

No part of this guidebook shall be reproduced in any form without permission in writing from the publisher except in the case of brief quotations embodied in critical articles or reviews.

Legal & Disclaimer

The information contained in this ebook is not designed to replace or take the place of any form of medicine or professional medical advice. The information in this ebook has been provided for educational & entertainment purposes only.

The information contained in this book has been compiled from sources deemed reliable, and it is accurate to the best of the Author's knowledge; however, the Author cannot guarantee its accuracy and validity and cannot be held liable for any errors or omissions. Changes are periodically made to this book. You must consult your doctor or get professional medical advice before using any of the suggested remedies, techniques, or information in this book.

Upon using the information contained in this book, you agree to hold harmless the Author from and against any damages, costs, and expenses, including any legal fees potentially resulting from the application of any of the information provided by this guide. This disclaimer applies to any damages or injury caused by the use and application, whether directly or indirectly, of any advice or information presented, whether for breach of contract, tort, negligence, personal injury, criminal intent, or under any other cause of action.

You agree to accept all risks of using the information presented inside this book. You need to consult a professional medical practitioner in order to ensure you are both able and healthy enough to participate in this program.

Table Of Contents

Chapter 1: What Exactly Is An Private Investigator? _____ 1

Chapter 2: What Is A Civil Investigator? _ 3

Chapter 3: Whom Would I Be Working For? _____ 15

Chapter 4: About The Job Teaching _____ 21

Chapter 5: Innvestigator's Rentice _____ 45

Chapter 6: Tricks Of Trade _____ 68

Chapter 7: George Bus And The Secret Government Cavern _____ 91

Chapter 8: Dying With Your Eyes Open 115

Chapter 9: Your Claim Is Refused _____ 138

Chapter 10: Citizen 4 And The Promises Of Usis _____ 163

Conclusion _____ 184

Chapter 1: What Exactly Is An Private Investigator?

I was at my desk, looking over the cracks in the ceiling. I hadn't seen an issue in a while and there was something that needed to be given before I could give it. As if in a dream the bombshell appeared in my office. Her eyes were as blue as those of the ocean, and legs that lasted for days. She was looking desperate in her eyes when she was taking on the second-hand desk with the phone that was on top of it. She looked up , and her big blues matched my blues.

"I'm sorry to say that I'm in need of your help. My husband has disappeared and my police officers don't appear to have any clues."

The P.I gumshoe Private Dick, detective, from Sam Spade to Mickey Spillane's Mike Hammer, private investigators have been appearing on the radio, the big, or small, for years. A number of authors have written about a variety of these gun-toting heroes through clever comments and humorous replies. It has resulted in many eager to take on the challenge but do you really know all the requirements for being an investigator for private companies? Are you even aware of the definition of a private investigator?

All in the title. Investigators are hired by private citizens or lawyers, as well as other organizations to discover the identity of a person, if the company can be trusted, and if they are being dishonest. Investigators are also employed to monitor expenditure in order to discover fraud, while others are able to track down missing and fugitives people. Are you paying attention to me now? Didn't you think there were many? There's more than you thought. Luckily, they can be broken down into two broad types, criminal and civil.

Chapter 2: What Is A Civil Investigator?

This is the investigator who completes all the dirty tasks for civil trials. Civil trials may range from personal injuries to custody dispute. Civil investigators are the person who gathers the evidence to argue a case during these trials. They are usually employed by companies, lawyers or spouses. Yes, I said spouses.

Have you ever wondered what the reliability of your babysitter or nanny actually is? Have you noticed that your children aren't thrilled about the arrival of their sitter? In this scenario the investigator will be able to conduct surveillance of your home, typically via electronic or if asked, follow the nanny or sitter through their routines to see whether your suspicions are right or if you're anxious about nothing. They will also conduct background checks of nannies, caregivers, and sitters. They are there to assist you in gaining security. They are able to conduct background checks on employees too.

Joey was injured at work and claims he injured himself. You are the one who is currently going through all the paperwork to ensure that he receives compensation but the injury, at least you thought it would, won't take that long to be healed. Joey is supposed to be back to exercise from the ankle strain after several weeks, isn't he? What is the reason he continues to claim that he is in discomfort after one month? Another reason why someone should employ an investigator. The investigator would monitor Joey to ensure that there is no injury and not taking advantage of the worker's compensation claim of everything it's worth.

A person fell in a grocery store, claiming there was a slippery substance on the floor. They did not see any signs that indicated there was a floor that was wet. They've visited a doctor, and are receiving treatment after deciding to file a lawsuit against the store. The store then employs an investigator for personal injuries to determine how the accident actually occurred, watch videofootage, and in many cases, contact neighbors and friends regarding the individual to determine whether the injury is genuine or if they're trying to make money. Personal injury lawsuits involve automobile accidents or pain and suffering or food poisoning.

It is possible that you are the kind of private investigator who is employed to examine financial documents. They are given the responsibility of searching through tax documents, deeds and other financial records to determine if the individual who is being investigated earns enough to support the lifestyle they lead or if they're making money off the top or, even more egregiously by stealing money from clients. These detectives can find mobster. These were the gumshoes which have caught Al Capone on tax evasion and Bernie Madoff on his Ponzi scheme.

Are you missing your loved ones and don't believe police are in the right direction? Are you worried that your child or son ran off, and you'd be willing to do anything to locate the missing person and bring them back? Civil agents can be of assistance in this regard, too. They are able to ask questions and monitor the timeframes, taking into consideration that certain people don't speak to police. They'll have the tools that they can use to determine the location where your loved ones were taken, or where they left. They're given more freedom than officers , and can tell when to be loud and when to be calm. They are able to spend more time to your case than an overwhelmed police department. They may not always provide the results you're looking for, but they'll keep you informed more frequently than the police department.

Of course, there is an additional challenge that this detective type. Civil gumshoes are typically hired to uncover dirt on a partner to prove their inability to act as the parent in custody cases. They also are employed to look into cases of abuse that involve children. This means that they must examine a family's or foster parents' lives to prove or disprove allegations of abuse or neglect. They must also monitor the parent at issue around to ensure that they're not leading an unsafe life to their family and children. Another benefit of a domestic detective that they also get to follow a spouse's trail to discover evidence, or lack of it of being unfaithful.

What exactly is a criminal investigator?

The act of committing insurance fraud, whether it's business or medical is a crime. It involves the false reporting of the medical treatments administered to the patient, or examining the premises of a commercial enterprise to determine if the harm caused was actually an outside source, or by the owner of the company. They are hired by insurance companies to conduct an independent investigation in order to decide if the award is worth paying or whether someone is guilty of fraud. You've seen these incidents on television, the news, and even on our big screens. These are cases of the person who takes out an insurance policy for someone they love, only to have the deceased person being discovered. Another instance would be an owner of a business who is in deep debt, and is setting the fire to his business to get the money to pay for his expenses. The job of a fraud investigator is to go on the scene, talk to the people whom the claimant is familiar with and look over the financial records and other historical documents to draw an image of either the victim who was unlucky or the person who was responsible for the offense.

Crime scene detectives reconstruct a crime scene order to understand the events that led to the events that occurred on the scene. They generally operate in teams, and even though the media would suggest they're gun-toting detectives in actual they are only using microscopes, ballistic gel and medical degrees that pertain to the area of investigation they conduct. A Medical Examiner does the in-depth investigation of a murder by examining the body for the cause of death, causeof death as well as other elements. One examiner analyzes dental impressions in the case of undetected bodies. There are even engineers who specialize in this area of investigation who study the possibility of recreating any event from an accident to a fire accident. The characters you see on television. The ones who enter the home to collect the details are called criminal scene inspectors. Similar to they are a part of the

M.E., they have to scrutinize, tag and record every item of evidence found at the site of the crime. They gather fingerprints, debris shoes prints, fingerprints, and many other images so that they may recreate the crime scene for the jury and judge.

Following the initial call After the kit is now collected and the photographs are taken, the work of the sexual crime detective is now in place. The task isn't an effortless task. It's not just the ability to understand the facts to identify the culprit, but they must also possess the skills of social interaction and compassion to speak and interact with victims. Sexual crimes can range from rape to stalking and everything in between. This isn't an easy task in any way. Investigators must look for clues, locate witnesses, and perform the research that nobody else would dare to complete. They must make sure the victim is not a victim and is not attempting to commit the crime. This is where the difficulty lies and one needs to be cautious. What are you able to do?

Being the victim of theft is unsettling. The police are called. They arrive ask you questions, along with crime scene experts gather evidence. Then they leave to create a report and then investigate the incident. This seems straightforward and you're wondering what the reason is for the need to engage a private investigator to investigate your case. Private investigators within this field would have an extensive network of contacts and an understanding of the best places for an investigation that would continue until you're completely satisfied. That means you have more chance of recovering your possessions.

Do you know someone who was kidnapped? While police are on the case or waiting for a message or call or a note, this detective can make use of evidence and move to areas where the police could be located to increase the odds of having an enjoyable ending. There are a variety of outcomes however, they typically work together with police officers to make sure that everything is in order however, they'll not stop until they have reached the end of the story.

This brings us to the reverse aspect of tracing people: skipping tracing. Also denoted by the name of Bounty Hunting, these investigators are employed by bond brokers to find those who were scheduled for an appointment with a judge, but chose not to attend. You can see on television channels taking down doors and rushing to businesses and homes to track down their suspect. Many types of criminal private investigations can be dangerous however none is more dangerous than bounty hunting. Inexpensive, armed, or desperate at the extreme cases Some of the fugitives have been in prison, and aren't planning on returning. They don't have anything to lose and they'll never give an second thought about shooting to kill someone who is on their trail. It requires tenacity, strength as well as street-smarts and the ability to master small-unit tactics to reduce the risk of being injured or killed. Bounty hunters typically operate in groups.

There are instances that an attorney may require someone to look into a case to improve the defense of his client. This is when an expert in defense comes into the scene. These gumshoes are hired , not just to review of the evidence and interviews that are not up to par and track the investigation but also to find flaws in the investigation, and look at evidence that may have been ignored. They collaborate with the defense lawyer to present the best defense possible to the person who is accused of the crime.

Criminal investigators are specialized in their training and access to more tools and resources that your normal civil police. They are equipped with the expertise to navigate the chain of custody in casesand keep evidence that could turn the direction of an investigation. They are required to adhere to the same procedures and laws that law enforcement follows, making sure that all evidence will be admissible in the court. In contrast to law enforcement and other law enforcement agencies, they will be working tirelessly to ensure that you are completely satisfied with the outcome. This means that they are able to assist in the resolution of more cases.

What Kind of Person Do I Want to be?

The next step is to decide what area you'd like to research. Certain specialists specialize in a single particular area, making them the top in their field. However due to their been specialized on a specific area, aside from those who hunt bounty, they compete with other professionals in the same field , and may have the possibility of slowing down. Other people choose a handful of areas, typically related fields that allow them to be employed. The final decision is yours to make.

You'll have to ask yourself what interests you the most. If you're an activist, then searching for missing persons, missing persons, ran-aways and getting to the root of the problem could be something you like to pursue. If you enjoy the excitement of hunting and the feeling of bringing an evil person to justice, then skip-tracing could be the right choice ideal for you. If you enjoy documents and solving mysteries by investigating the trail of paper, conducting background checks or determining whether someone is modifying financial records, then a Forensic investigator is right suitable for you. If you are a fan of following clues and aid in solving big crimes or crimes, then working with lawyers to prepare for court proceedings could be a good fit the right fit for you. There are numerous ways to go.

Chapter 3: Whom Would I Be Working For?

What you do for a company is contingent on the specifics of the situation, your specificities, and the particular situation. Fraud or embezzlement, family law and other similar cases can result in court proceedings that means you'll be employed by lawyers. If you're an expert in one of the areas of criminal law and you're likely to be working for a lawyer too. If you're focusing on domestic matters, run-aways divorces, or child abuse and so on, your employer could be your spouse or attorney. Insurance companies will hire you if they feel that an individual claim requires investigation, and they do not require the involvement of the police or even at the beginning. Corporate companies will put retained you to conduct background checks and , in rare instances, examine an employees' actions that they feel aren't in the best interest of the law.

If you're curious about what it will pay, that's usually dependent on you and the area you select. There are expenses and man-hours. It is important take all of this into consideration, or else you'll struggle to meet your financial goals even when you're doing the things you love. Consider the gumshoes you saw on the radio and television. They didn't really make a lot did they?

Your Education and Background...

The majority of investigators have been law enforcement in the past, with former military personnel coming in a close second however, this doesn't mean you won't be one. Some have forensic background already, and some have gotten into investigation through work in an forensic lab or the Medical Examiner's Office.

Ex-law enforcement personnel would probably be ex-detective as well as an officer. They may have retired from the force or walked out for different reasons, but would like to help people. There were some adjustments they needed to make in their tactics. In the end, they can not ask questions anymore or have to wait for warrants of search. They aren't able to carry their badges no more. They'd have to come up with alternative ways of uncovering information to get to the root of the issue.

Former military personnel who go in the field appreciate the long hours and the results, however they also are in a transitional phase. They need to establish an image and establish contacts and research the places they could explore further and then learn how to interact with others for the answers they require. A majority of these avoid tracing people who are missing or lost.

There are people who possess degrees in the field of criminology. This provides them with an advantage but they require additional training in different areas and must build skills that can aid in achieving results. They'll be more skilled at figuring out the motives behind the case they're hired. They'll also be better competent in interpreting the data and evidence, however this doesn't mean they are an investigator. Their experience makes them an investigator.

In order to be an investigator, you need to be persistent as well as tenacious and self-motivated in achieving results. You'll be your personal boss, but you have to be able to please your client. It's not possible when you're not motivated by your own self. It is also essential to have a an eye for small nuances and details that could lead you to your culprit or be the cause in the event that you are working. You must be trustworthy. Your reputation is not just be based on the outcomes you've had, but on how reliable, responsive and trustworthy you appear. You may be a top investigator, but if do not keep in contact with the clienton a regular basis, explore all angles, and document your the progress, you will not be able to get positive reviews or gain new clients, let alone return clients.

If you're one of those who would like to learn how to become an investigator, but have no prior enforcement, law enforcement, or military background, choosing the right school will be the most important factor to success. Choose an institution that offers all aspects of investigations. This would include:

"Navigating around the Law

o How to operate in accordance with the law to maintain your license. What are your rights within the law and how you can gather evidence that is admissible in an in-court of law.

* Where to search for information,

It will require online searches as well as libraries and accessing the company's documents.

It also explains how to combine all the information into a short and understandable report.

* Surveillance techniques,

It includes background checks, following an individual suspect, locating them and also how to identify an individual.

* The equipment required to conduct an investigation

* How to collaborate in conjunction with Homeland Security and other law enforcement organizations.

It also provides instructions on how to work undercover and the process of removing corporate spying

- Interviewing techniques; finger prints analysis and handwriting analysis, as well as firearms training.

* How to advertise yourself as a private detective.

You'll also have to obtain a license. The best school will assist you get your investigative license as well as your firearm license. If you want to carry a concealed firearm it is necessary to obtain an authorization for that too.

Chapter 4: About The Job Teaching

Mike was an outstanding private investigator. Mike was diligent, patient and meticulous. Mike is a pro at surveillance. He was a keen cyclist during his leisure time, and brought that same determination and perseverance to the field of investigation. The place he was raised was Hamilton, Montana, in the picturesque Bitterroot Valley under the Sapphire Mountains. He relocated from Montana to Houston, Texas, after having graduated at his school, the University of Montana, Missoula. Lucian Burke was an older and more sarcastic private detective who had offices across Texas. He recruited his assistant to assist him. Lucian was able to convince Mike to establish an office in San Antonio office. This is where I began working on workers' compensation surveillance as well as insurance defense monitoring. A case of insurance defense that involved Paul Skerritt, an avid football fan from a small town, suffering from an injury to his lower back, was among my first surveillance projects.

According to some sources, the top three religions in Texas include football, and soccer. This isn't an exaggeration I can guarantee that to. Football is a major sport on all levels. Texas has two football clubs that are professional: The Dallas Cowboys and the Texas A&M Aggies. They've had a performance record that includes eight Super Bowl trips and five wins. The rivalry in college football that exists between Texas A&M Aggies and the University of Texas Longhorns is popular and has been going on since.

1894[25]. The game begins with the school-level. Football is the top sport throughout all of the states, from largest cities to the tiniest of communities. It was also the case at La Vernia (a small community located 30 miles to the to the east San Antonio). Around one thousand residents.

The son of Paul Duke was an offensive tight end for the football team at high school, La Vernia Bears. Duke was an exceptionally talented player. Paul was very proud to become the father of his son. Paul did not miss any game. Paul was extremely obsessive about football. It's remarkable considering this was Texas. He was a fervent football enthusiast. He would always show his foam fingers to anyone and shout "We're the best!" to everyone and anyone. While Duke was initially shocked by the antics that his dad was known for, he quickly became a household name in the town.

Paul was injured in a car crash. Paul was suffering from extreme lower back pain that rendered him unable to work or perform other tasks. For the purpose of determining if further monitoring was required, I conducted an activity test. This was a half-day of surveillance. Paul didn't do anything during the check for activity. However, I conducted some small-scale inquiries in the area and discovered that Paul was attending Duke's football game on Friday night.

match. I wrote down a mental note to attend.

Paul was a fervent football fan, but I had no idea about. After nearly 30 years of business I have found nothing that astonishes me. At about 5:00 on a Friday, I put up a surveillance system near Paul's house and parked my car in the direction Paul is likely to quit the area. It proved that I didn't have to wait for long. He made his way to his vehicle from the driveway just after the hour of 6:00 pm. It is essential to witness the whole thing. Paul was about five feet eight inches tall and weighed about 200 pounds. He had white sneakers, white pants and an La Vernia Bears blue football jersey. He was his child Duke was the name in the shirt, which was adorned with the number 34. In the Texas sun's flat I could clearly see the white face of his, and his hair was vibrant blue. He also carried his finger that was foam. As he drove towards the parking lot, I accompanied him , laughing as we drove towards the football stadium at the high school.

It's not easy to follow someone in crowds. Paul's outfit meant that I could be observant of his movements as we moved through the stadium. I ended up five rows back of him and a little further to the left. The rest of the crowd saw me as a fan with camera. Any person who was observant enough could see the camera I used was directed towards Paul and not towards the field.

Paul noticed a dramatic personality change when the game began. Paul started screaming and jumping around in every game. Although I'm not a physician It appears it was the case that pain caused by his lower back injury was gone. I continued filming while he was behind. The film was close to being finished when I had finished the video. Paul is seen climbing the stadium steps. Paul is seen walking down the stairs of the stadium. Paul is found walking sideways across the bleachers. Paul is flailing his arms, and wave his arms. Paul is bent forward, throwing himself up and down. Paul even made the wave. Paul performed every physical activity that wasn't directly related to his back. I thought about it for the entire evening: I was paid to go to football games as well as eat hot dogs as well as filming a guy who had blue eyes. This isn't something you can make up.

Paul's insurance defense case isn't unusual. In the following three years, I'll continue to take on hundreds in similar situations. Paul is just one of the many plaintiffs who exaggerate their injuries in order to collect as much as they can when the claim is resolved. There is a serious fraudster when you add untruthful chiropractors, corrupt lawyers and untrustworthy doctors. It's a rogue business that costs $7 billion a year to fraud. Private investigator: I work as an investigator for an insurance company. My role is to observe the claimant's progress to assess the severity the extent of injuries. My job is to determine if the claimant's activities in their daily lives fall within the range of their injuries. My role is to help the insurance company to negotiate an equitable settlement. I don't make any recommendations, make adjudications or pass judgement. I just gather information. The truth is often in the middle. It's usually somewhere in between. Many of these individuals have been legitimately injured. They're not as hurt in the way they say. Another case I was involved in was fraud in workers' compensation. I was part of an investigation of Ben Stockton (a bus driver from Austin Texas).

Ben was a resident of Green Mills in Austin's older section, close to The University of Texas. It was the end of summer and I was seated in my vehicle for surveillance in the shade of the huge Huisache tree. To let the cool breeze to flow through my van I had to lower the windows a few inches. While male cicadas beat their tymbales to draw females from the species I was able to hear them sing. In a nearby house there was a person cutting their lawn. I could smell fresh cut grass. I sat in awe, in anticipation of my question to be answered.

Ben Stockton, a tall man who suffered a back injury, the lower back area, was employed by workers compensation. Stockton was only five feet tall, yet his weight was more than 350 pounds. It always struck me as ironic me that a lot of my clients with back injuries were also overweight. There was probably a connection. The doctor who treated Stockton said that Stockton was so ill that he could not sit or stand for long durations of time. Stockton could not bend or lift more than 10 pounds. Stockton was evidently in unhealthy health. He was so ill that he skipped the weekly appointments for physical therapy. The red light was sent to the adjuster taking care of the case. I was there to visit the situation at his home. It was my job to find out whether the actions of Stockton, just like Paul Skerritt's, were in line with the injuries he claimed to have suffered.

The Stockton family and wife had left me just two days ago. There was no trace of him at present. Private eyes are usually capable of speculating about the location of the person or that the person is not at the address. It's not uncommon for people to watch for hours at the home of the suspect and then discover that it's been abandoned. Or, it's the wrong home. I looked up the plates on the vehicles in the driveway, and they all of them were from Stockton. I was able to locate the right home. I took my time. John Connolly, an Irish writer who wrote about it once, said: "We all have our routines...but they must serve an objective. They should have an end result that we can see and be content with. They're nothing but the endless pacing of caged animal 26[. I understood the quote as an indication that Stockton will eventually need to leave the enclosure. I'd be prepared if Stockton was to go outside.

Third day monitoring was the most difficult. I finally spotted something I'd never noticed before. A front entrance would be opened at 10:00 AM and then at 1:00 pm each day. The large Airedale Terrier, with long black and brown hair walked into the yard to conduct business. After he was done with his stroll through the yard and walked to an undetermined point to take a bath. Then the dog walked through his yard till he arrived at his destination. The dog's Master, Stockton, then whistled and the dog returned to his comfortable home. Even though I'd observed the dog for the previous 2 days, I was unable to pay enough attention. I was unaware that he entered the home from inside. I assumed that it was a dog from the neighborhood. Stockton was able to accomplish this without making a fuss about his presence. It made the job difficult. It was the same situation until the next day when the dog refused entrance.

The same incident occurred the next day, exactly at 10:07 in the morning. Stockton requested the great beast to enter at the correct time. But, he wasn't in a position to enter. Stockton continued to ignore his master while the animal ran and played on the lawn in front. I knew it was to my advantage. My camera was pointed to the entrance, then zoomed into, and started my video camera. Then I became Captain Ahab looking forward to my white whale to appear.

Silence. Nothing. The cool breeze was akin to my neck. Thin layers of sweat gradually ran across my forearm. A small sounds of garbage truck advancing at a distance could be heard. The hound was a great one and the front door was left open. I stood there. He began to whistle. He was silent. The end was near! Stockton suddenly showed up, and I hit record on my camera. Stockton was attentively looking across the street and his eyes were moving between left and to the right. He was looking, but not looking at anything. He then walked out into his front garden with his feet still in bare.

He was wearing worn-out brown cargo pants as well as an San Antonio Spurs white t-shirt. Stockton believed that Stockton wanted to play was moving toward Stockton and fled to the opposite end of the field. I continued filming video and meticulously document each step. Stockton ran around, swerved, and dipped as Stockton was swerving, running and bent over. Stockton also ran in a sideways direction and jumped around the dog for an additional ten minutes. Stockton tried everything to capture the dog. His physical activity was in complete contradiction to his physical and bodily limitations. Stockton seemed to be in perfect health and had no problem. Stockton was more apparent when he sped through the streets at full speed and then took his dog of fifty pounds, and then returned him to his house.

I brought my camera along and set the car seat to an appropriate height and then put the transmission into drive. I slowly changed the steering column and I left the scene. Then, mentally, I checked Ben Stockton off of my list. There were a lot of instances of insurance fraud. About 30 percent of all workers' compensation claims involve fraud. As per the Coalition Against Insurance Fraud (CAIF), Paul Skerritt, Ben Stockton and other fraudsters cost taxpayers $80 billion annually. We are left wondering why insurance premiums have gone up so much. It was evident that I had plenty of work to complete. Maybe the guy next to me owned an animal?

While Ben and Paul's instances were involving fraudulent workers' compensation as well as personal injury fraud that are two distinct kinds of insurance fraud They are both instances of soft fraud, or opportunity theft in the way that the insurance industry calls them. This occurs when a law-abiding person exaggerates the amount of insurance coverage that is generally legitimate. It's funny to watch people fabricate false information to make more cash from insurance firms. It's part in the "everybody is doing the same thing" mentality. This isn't something that everybody does. It's only that everybody is ultimately paying. It's likely that many of my cases of insurance fraud were in these areas of uncertainty.

In the next few days, I began being employed by Mike Farmer five to six days a week as a security officer during college classes. I had time to read. My work schedule included holidays and weekends. Private investigator, I've been employed on every holiday, except for Christmas Day. I was in the field from late afternoon until late at night and was generally in the office before 6 am. My first training session lasted about two weeks. It included a ride along with Stuart Hall, Mike's senior investigator, and the most experienced. Stu was a nice person. He was slim, tall and beautiful. It made him appear like an Hollywood star. Stu comes from Kerrville in Texas which is a tiny town located on the banks of on the Guadalupe River, located in the Texas Hill Country about an hour to the north to San Antonio. While Stu tried to assist me, the first couple of weeks were a bit blurred. I was mostly accountable for making notes and asking questions as Stu carried out surveillance. Although Stu was a great investigator, I soon realized that surveillance is something that can only be learned through practicing it. When I began working on my own I found that there are some things that you could only learn through trial and error. That's how I view making mistakes. I've made many mistakes.

I made nearly every error I could make in my initial few months of monitoring. My subject was never found. I was burned [27] a number of times. One time, I hit the car's sound system with my rear end when I moved from the driver's seat to the rear. Since I was in a standing position of surveillance that appeared out of place, police were forced to contact me. People in my neighborhood came up to me and offered assistance. One neighbor even offered me a refreshing soft drink. He claimed that it was humid for me leave the house doing what it was I did. I was incorrectly addressed many times and my headlights weren't switched on numerous times, even after daylight savings time started. In all it was not my most enjoyable time of the day.

I once went with two elderly people from South San Francisco.

Antonio to attend a North San Antonio physical therapy appointment. They did not get stuck in traffic, and I managed to do it amazingly. My efforts were an honor for me. They took the car out and stopped to park. I looked up at them and they smiled and smiled and waved. In my normal way I nearly waved at them.

Another occasion I set up surveillance in an apartment complex located on Fredericksburg Road. My subject was a member of in the Hell's Angels [28] motorcycle club. He sped out his front entrance, and I didn't stay for longer than twenty minutes. He was huge tall, standing six feet tall and weighing at 3000 pounds. The entire thing was muscle. While he was walking along my route, I noticed that he held his right hand in open position and was carrying his gun. It was a strange coincidence that he was heading toward me. When I gazed through the camera's lens it became evident that he was going directly towards me. I started the engine then put it into drive. After I got out of the garage, the tires shook as well as laid tread. The tires weren't working.

Mike was extremely patient. Mike was a professional who knew the need to gain knowledge from other researchers. He was correct. Slowly, I improved. I made mistakes and learned from them. As time passed, my abilities were greatly improved. I became proficient in the field of the art of surveillance, that I had been able to identify my subjects in the act of committing fraud. Mike started calling my overall success "Fulmer luck." Seneca was the Roman Philosopher, said, "Luck is what happens when the preparation is met with the right opportunity." I definitely had plenty. It was a healthy goal to raise like in the case of Diego Ramirez. [29]

Diego was said to have injured his back when he was working as a barback. Pun intended. He was getting an annual workers' compensation check , but there was a possibility that he was employed. Workers' compensation can be a means to be compensated as the person recovers from an injury sustained at work. Diego was believed of the adjuster for claims that he was working off the side. I pretexted Diego. I contacted him to inform him how I was referred to him to him by a close friend. He was attending an event for private parties, and I learned that it was a bartender. It was clear that he was looking for the position. When he agreed I informed me that I had to meet him at the bar prior to hiring him. He wasn't the person I wanted to work with and there was nothing that was. The goal of the call was to determine where he was employed, and in violation of the workers' compensation rules. He stated that he was in Casa Rio on Friday night the popular Mexican restaurant on the Riverwalk in downtown San Antonio. I said I'd visit after 8:00 pm in order to greet him.

It was one of the very first times Valerie had ever collaborated on a case me. Friday came and we walked through downtown San Antonio to Riverwalk. One story lower than street level and the San Antonio River (or Paseo del Rio) gradually flows and flows through the downtown area of San Antonio. Both banks are lined with restaurants of high-end cuisine as well as art galleries and tourist shops. The river is surrounded by fifty foot Bald Cypress trees that provide shade and shade. It's a relaxing and festive setting. The Riverwalk is the second-highest-visited tourist attraction, following the Alamo. The Riverwalk draws more than 12 million people each year, and spends around $2 billion. Conventions and conferences of all kinds are held each year at the luxurious hotels near the river.

Casa Rio is situated on the Riverwalk and is located situated between Commerce Street & W. Market Street. The business is owned by a family which serves TexMex food since 1945. The white napkins are used by waiters. They serve big drinks with salty kosher in large glasses. They also serve an assortment of succulent steak fajitas as well as the frozen margaritas made with lime. Mariachis dressed in classic dark Charro suit [30] walk the dining room and play folk music from Mexico. The

Riverwalk provides dining al fresco in its various eateries, with tables set close to the riverbanks. Casa Rio is no exception.

There was still a lot of humidity in the river but there was a soft breeze blowing gently across it despite the humidity. The sound of the water running across the riverbank was all I could hear along with the steady sound of a motor while the Riverwalk boat slowed. While the tour guide shared the history of the area, visitors sailed along on the San Antonio River from the tiny barge. Some tables were large banquets that were covered with linen tables and guests were able to enjoy Tex-Mex meals with candles. Valerie and I arrived just at the same time as Valerie was already in the room. I could hear the conversation, feel the glasses clanging, and feel the fresh aroma of flour tortillas with cut spicy pico. I spotted Diego immediately. I noticed him in the back of the bar and, despite the temperatures, he was sweating profusely in Texas. I persuaded the hostess to put us in a place with a stunning view of the back of the bar. There was no doubt that the Riverwalk was a popular tourist destination and every table had cameras. This was prior to smartphones and video applications. My video camera was in my face alongside my hot chicken enchiladas Verdes. I cautiously pointed it at Diego's direction and began to shoot video. Valerie and I sat down and enjoyed our meal as the camera was doing all the work. Diego looked at me several times and Valerie appeared to believe we were watching him. However, I did not provide him with any reason to think that I was suspicious. I was just a tourist taking a bite to eat with cameras.

I was able capture about an hour of Diego bent over, carrying heavy plastic crates packed with glasses that were clean. He was often bent to get a cooler around his waist, behind the bar and kept working far beyond the limits of his injury. This was the end of it. It may surprise you to learn that it's not always easy to identify clues in the investigation process. Diego was working an extremely physically demanding job, as well as receiving a pay check from workers Compensation. While my video isn't sexually explicit, it did do the job. After viewing my video, the claims adjuster requested Diego to undergo a physical exam by a physician. After viewing the video the doctor conducted an examination on Diego. The doctor released Diego for return to work. Case dismissed.

Valerie as well as my husband Dylan were blessed with three sons when I left the Army to go to college. Our first child was Brandon and was followed by Dylan and, finally, our youngest child, Alyssa which is our sole child. Valerie was the one who spent the most time taking care of the kids while I worked full-time at college. It was tough for us both and especially Valerie. Dylan was in good health, however Brandon has Asperger's Disease[3]It is a neurobiological disorder which is now known as High-Functioning Autism. Alyssa was born with spina bifida; specifically, Tethered Cord Syndrome; Lipomyelomeningocele, a very rare birth defect that affects the spine and often has neurological consequences. When she was just three months old she underwent her first operation. She had seven additional operations before becoming twelve. Alyssa along with me have witnessed numerous miracles in her health. When she was a baby it was suggested that Alyssa undergo the first operation for removing the cord of her spinal spine. We were fortunate that we were located in San Antonio at the time. It was here that the doctors Dr. Sara J. Gaskill along with Dr. Arthur E. Marlin were practising medical practice. It was discovered that these two world-renowned neurosurgeons who were pediatrics developed the medical instruction manual for the exact type of operation Alyssa required. Valerie and I sat in a waiting area, in a solitary state, and terrified, as two of the most innovative surgeons performed delicate surgeries on our infant girl in 1997. We were assisted by a lady from the spina Bifida support group. This was by far the longest waiting time in my whole life.

The harsh truth was that my two kids were both born with birth defects that were rare. I've never been a fan about the word. It was mystifying to me for many years whether this was because of my exposure to chemical or nerve substances throughout this Gulf War. It was known to everyone that Saddam Hussein had weapons of mass destruction (32), which was among the primary reasons why it was that the U.S. entered war with Iraq. The weapons were also used to fight the Kurds, Iran, and other nations. This is an established fact. However, I was curious. The unit I was in soon moved to the northern part of Iraq close to and around the Ar Rumaylah Oil Field. The move took place in January and February 1991 during the same time it was during this time that the U.S. attacked Iraq's weapons factories and storage facilities. A large number of U.S. soldiers were infected by the noxious clouds that hung over Iraq which infected them with various signs later known as Gulf War Syndrome. I recall being told to utilize my MOPP[33] equipment more often than I remember throughout the month of January and February in 1991. Six years later two of my children were born with neurologic birth defects. My children are an inspiration and enrich my life.

A lot of people believe Saddam did not have the weapons that could cause mass destruction. It is possible that he had them but he could not have. Maybe it was remnants of his battle in the war against Kurds and the Iranians. I'm not sure. Gulf War Syndrome is a condition that affects around 25% of the total 697,000 military personnel who participated in the war of 1991. The illness is believed to cause more than a third of the soldiers who were involved in wartime operations. I was wondering if it could have affected Brandon, me Brandon and Alyssa.

My research did not involve fine Tex-Mex food and a dinner on Riverwalk with my beloved. A lot of what you see on television isn't quite so interesting as it appears. Sometimes, it's boring. It takes a lot concentration and patience to keep track of someone's movements. In my case, for instance, I might sit for hours gazing at my subject's front door but only be able to record two minutes of video as the mailbox is opened. It is important to be ready for the two minutes. Even though it could only take two minutes, in some cases it's enough.

Chapter 5: Innvestigator's Rentice

It all began in Phyllis Williams in her late 60s, a taller woman with shorter grey hair. Her curvaceous face was enhanced by her attractive appearance. She was wearing the identical orange shorts and white t-shirt everyday while she worked hard in her flower gardens. She was not married after her husband's death a few years in the past. She was a very busy person, who spent most times in the garden and observing what was happening in the neighborhood. Though she believed she was an honest citizen, many of her people in the neighborhood saw her disruptive actions in their lives as interference with their personal affairs. She would spend hours mowing her front yard until no blade of grass was left unattended. Phyllis was able to observe the activities and occurrences that her neighbours were experiencing from their at a certain point. She would betray the neighbors who were infractions to minor provisions of the city's code of conduct and call the dog trapper to report any wandering dogs. No one was allowed to sit on their lawns, or let their grass get too long. Phyllis was always there to remind them when they did.

Private investigation is a popular business that uses informants and people who snitch. Phyllis was a very busy woman however her snooping was able to save Rosie as well as Cherry Jordan from their hubris and uncontrollable greed. Theirs was the sole mother and daughter team I've ever witnessed in the field of insurance fraud.

Rosie and Cherry like many instances of insurance defence, started out legally injured. They then began to profit from their position, similar to other fraudsters. This meant they over exaggerated their injuries, and then dragged out their settlement to obtain as much money as they could in settlement. Cherry and Rosie were involved injured in an incident. They weren't the ones to blame. The utility company's truck in Dallas County hit them. Rosie was unable to pay an utility firm's medical expenses. Although she was a first name, her attitude wasn't the most pleasant. She was always complaining about the fact about how Cherry her daughter and herself, had suffered serious injuries. Both were fortunate to be alive. That's the reason! She was looking for a new car. She wanted to earn more money. She was looking for to see a different doctor. Although her injuries weren't serious she complained of a decrease in group [34].

Rosie's silent complaints remained unabated for months. Each week, she called an adjuster for claims. The claims adjuster was so irritable to work with, so much that the adjuster of the utility company pleaded with Rosie she hire an attorney aid her. Rosie declared she was not planning to give her money to an attorney who sucks blood.

Stephen Hawking, an English theoretical physicist, once wrote that "it is ineffective to get unhappy over your disability...People do not be able to appreciate you they are constantly angry and complaining." This is one thing that Rosie and Cherry ought to have learnt. It was discovered that their neighbor next door, Phyllis had the most trouble and was not a fan to listen to their complaints.

Rosie said something that upset Phyllis some time prior to the incident. It was so long ago that Phyllis was unable to recall the specifics. However, she did remember that feeling of having been kicked out by Rosie the day. She held on to the feeling. She was taking charge of it. She looked after it until it became an adult-sized anger. She was waiting to compensate since. Rosie spoke about the car crash to Phyllis and added "I'm going to take the firm for every dime they've got!"

Phyllis has seen Rosie as well as her baby girl and decided that their injuries weren't serious. She had a chance to get her revenge. She took advantage of the chance. She took her phone and dialed the utility company. She repeated verbatim the words Rosie had stated. Their insurance company was contacted to by their utility provider. The insurance company called me.

I began my investigation and was able to find out very quickly the details Phyllis was aware of. Rosie and Cherry her daughter, who is 17 years old was healthy and well-behaved despite the incident. Their injuries weren't as serious as they appeared. Cherry is also the top player on her volleyball team at high school, in addition, Rosie was her most ardent fan. Cherry was a student at Arlington High School. I stumbled across an Arlington High School website and phoned a couple of times. I was able to locate the volleyball schedule and discovered it was Cherry's Lady Colts Varsity Volleyball Team will be playing Gophers Grand Prairie High School Gophers on Friday. Like Paul Skerritt did, I was there with my camera.

I am to Arlington High School on Friday at just the right time for at 6:30 p.m. game. I grabbed an ice cold Dr. Pepper, a hot dog topped with spicy mustard, and freshly chopped onion , and moved up to the top of the bleachers. I found a comfy place at the end of the visitor's side. I enjoyed the most spectacular views. I was able to record Cherry lying on the flooring, as well as Rosie in the opposing bleachers. It was as if every person in the stands had their own camera. It was similar to Diego Ramirez's surveillance of the Riverwalk in San Antonio. I sat down, ate my meal, and then took footage of Cherry and Rosie before everyone else. I was pleased to be a parent with camera.

Although I had seen an unintentional video of Rosie prior to the game, Cherry became my very first time with her. It was awe-inspiring to see how thin and tall she was. She was a strong, tall lady with extremely long legs. Her body was ideal for playing volleyball. Her straight, long brunette hair was tied into ponytails and secured by a white ribbon. She then leapt high to deliver a massive jump serve. Cherry fell to the ground, and then quickly rose up, extensing her toned, slender arms to set the ball to her partner. You can watch it on the video. Cherry was absolutely smashed, but I'm not saying brutally smashed by the opposition team. Every spike was followed by the blood-curdling sound of a high-pitched, high-pitched. The grunts brought memories of my days in the bayonet class in Ft. Benning's Infantry School. The crowd was awestruck each time Cherry performed this. Cherry was cheered on across the entire gymnasium. The girl was gifted. The entire thing was recorded on video.

Rosie was in the bleachers watching my performance. Rosie would leap around and down every time Cherry did something extraordinary. It was not uncommon. She would also shout and raise her arms over her head. She would then begin clapping and then turn her head to the crowd , and then nod her head in a way to announce that she was their daughter. The whole evening was spent looking toward the bleachers as well as Cherry and then back to Rosie.

Because of the video evidence I found, Rosie & Cherry did not win the substantial financial gain they had hoped for. They were forced to settle their claims. The settlement was far less as well as more realistic to with their injuries as opposed to their exaggerated claims. Rosie may also be thankful for her friend Phyllis who was asking questions over the deal. It's obvious that you do not know who is paying attention. It's impossible to have a clue who to trust.

I was drawn to this job because each day was unique. I don't sit at an office. This isn't an all-time 8-hour workday. It's not my style. I'm not sure what the coming step might bring. I'm not certain what will get when I pick up the phone. It usually starts with an actual phone call in life. Similar to the time I received an email about the absence of tortillas.

The shocking disappearance of thousands hundreds of dollars' worth of Mexican food items in Caliente Sabroso Foods, Houston, Texas was the great tortilla theft. The missing tortillas and taco shells were the primary reason for the robbery. Also, there were bottles of salsa. Jalapenos. This isn't the case with a few tortillas made from flour and one jar salsa. It's greater than $20,000.00 in product that is missing.

Caliente Sabroso Foods, a major wholesale distributor of Mexican foods to stores of all sizes and restaurants across in the Southwest United States, is Caliente Sabroso Foods. Raul Estrada, a family from Mexico established the business in 1949. From the family's Magnolia

Park home, which was near Houston's shipping channel, the family started making delicious pork tamales as well as flour tortillas. They began selling them to their neighbors, friends and their colleagues. The business began to expand rapidly. It gradually grew to become a multimillion-dollar business that sold more than 30 types of goods. They operate from a manufacturing plant as well as a number of warehouses situated on the east of Houston close to Interstate Highway 10. Rocky Sepulveda, their senior facility manager, was on hand in one of their facilities for food production.

Rocky was an Hispanic man who was less than 5'6 inches tall with shorter brunette hair, and a firm handshake. Rocky was wearing western boots, and starched Levi's as well as an oversized western shirt. A white haircover from the industrial era was affixed to his head. After he had given me the tour of their factory I was handed one.

Rocky was able figure that Caliente Sabroso's inventory was lacking about two pallets every week. It was about $3,000.00 worth of Mexican food each week. It was a tiny amount, and was not noticed for several weeks until it was discovered to be an anomaly in a monthly audit. He estimated that they were carrying around $10,000.00 in the product. It was not a lot when you consider how much Caliente Sabroso made each year. It was also a sign that someone was stealing from the company. Rocky determinedly tried to stop the thief.

Rocky and I went on an inspection of the warehouse. We discussed the security of the warehouse as well as inventory management. Although the warehouse was secured with cameras, they weren't up-to-date. In addition, the cameras failed to spot the major dead spots I discovered. The warehouse did not have an alarm system, and crucial control procedures were complicated. This was a surprise considering the size of the business and its resources. Rocky's explanation led me think that it was an insider's job. It was possible that somebody had made an additional key, and was returning late at night to load the product. Then

I went to Rocky and returned in the workplace to get myself ready for what was going to be a late night surveillance. surveillance. I recharged my camera and then put the equipment in the

Every night, the warehouse shuts at 9:00 pm, depending on the time each truck leaves. I snatched an ice-cold Dr. Pepper and sat down at my desk, trying discern the thoughts of those or people who were adding inventory. I thought that the employee returned a couple of hours after to continue their plunder. Jupiter Jones, author of The Three Investigators is a believer in Occam's Razor[3535. The scientific theory states that when there are many possibilities to explain a problem, The most probable explanation will be one that has the lowest probability explanation. Caliente Sabroso Foods would be without two pallets a week. The culprits could have utilized a truck or van to move the product. They might even be able to store the items in their storage. Nobody ever takes this much Mexican food. It's likely that the thieves offered it to smaller mom-and-pop

Mexican restaurant chains in Houston for just pennies per head.

At first I was conducting monitoring at various times, and at night. I carried on this for approximately an entire week but without any success. This is what happens with monitoring. Rocky and I both started becoming impatient after week 2. The irony is that since the multi-million dollar business wouldn't purchase the installation of an alarm or improve their security cameras. They were reluctant to find out about a burglary. It occurred like it was an ordinary thing. It was only happening at night.

It occurred shortly at midnight on the night of a Wednesday in November. The warehouse was shut for just under three hours. The warehouse was shut down for 3 hours due to the full moon and there was a cooling breeze coming from Trinity Bay. It was creeping up slowly getting into. It was almost silent. The place was silent, with only the occasional car that passed by along the roads nearby.

Strategically, I'd put myself in an unoccupied structure located next to Caliente Sabroso's store. When I first saw the man, I had already walked away from the windows and to the shadows. In a flash I felt my muscles contract when a male figure emerged from the fog and started walking towards me. I looked up, then re-examined them. It was not an apparition. He continued walking slowly toward the warehouse. He walked up the steps near the main dock for loading before stopping near the front door into the storage facility. He turned and stared at me. My heart jumped. I couldn't even make out his face. He turned his attention to me from the opposite direction before turning his back towards the door. I was able to watch him remove a set of keys from his pockets. When he put them in the locked compartment, a ray of moonlight pierced across the fog. I quickly picked up my phone to dial to re-dial. This was before text messaging was even possible via cell phones. Mario Salazar, another investigator for Mike Farmer, was hiding in the warehouse. Mario was the first to answer the phone.

"One Man," I replied. "He's on the way right now."

He swiftly said, "Got it", and then left. Mario continued to work in the warehouse for about 30 minutes. From his hideout he took video of the plunderer as he scurried across the walls to stay away from security cameras. The suspect was able to maneuver the forklift without being visible in security footage.

Mario was fighting the thief from within when I saw the headlights of a pair coming toward me from the fog on one side of the street. They appeared at first like they were disembodied, as if floating in the fog. They abruptly changed direction and started moving towards me. I finally saw the shape of the vehicle. It was a tiny U-Haul cargo vehicle in orange with an unidentified driver. The tires were pushing through the rainwater that was dripping from an earlier cold shower at night. When the U-Haul drove through the parking lot the driver released an intense, high-pitched noise as the truck stopped the front of the dock for loading. The driver shut down the lights on his head. I heard a metallic sound when the transmission was put in reverse. The driver then made the steering wheel turn in an arc, and pulled the vehicle towards the ramp to load. He then stepped out of the cab and started walking toward the rear of the truck where he took the bumper. I wasn't able to see him, but I could hear his familiar sound when he opened the UHaul's back cargo doors.

Bandit number 1 had entered the door to the warehouse from inside. Mario along with me recording the event on video. We also recorded close-ups of the faces of the bandits. It was a familiar sound coming from the forklift, and I was able to watch the first bandit take two pallets full of Mexican food items in the U-Haul. The driver locked the door and both men got in the truck to head out. I followed them until my vehicle, maintaining the distance to a safe level. They were just two miles away from the warehouse and so I took them on a walk. They stopped in front of a random home. I captured footage of the driver exiting, and he said goodbye. The video also included one of the shots that was taken from a close-up when he was standing under the light of his front porch. I took the driver to his residence and recorded another video while he parked his UHaul just on top of the residence. I made note of their addresses, both men and returned to collect Mario. We drove to the nearby 24 hour Whataburger and exchanging notes.

The same situation was repeated on Wednesday night, just after midnight. The men weren't creative. They returned on Wednesday. The company was ready for this time. Officers and detectives from the Houston Police Department jumped out of their vehicles, guns drawn in order to take down the thieves as they were stealing.

Caliente Sabroso Foods, like many other businesses, wanted to stay clear of negative publicity, so the incident wasn't reported by the press. My part as a witness was private. It was discovered that both bandits were employees. They were well-liked by all and one had even been a shift supervisor who was the one with the keys for the store. They were selling food items at mom-and-pop Mexican eateries in Houston at a cost of pennies per dollar, just as I previously predicted. They were buying the product at no cost for them. They made a profits. It was $20,000.00 worth of product that was not used double what Rocky initially thought.

When the supervisor was taking an off, he took a bite of a balony supper and thinking about all the things wrong with his life. The closed-circuit cameras covering the warehouse weren't covering the area, which he noticed. The cameras were old, cheaper cameras that were not sensitive to low-light. After a bit of digging and investigation, he discovered that these cameras recorded on an 8-day loop. This means that the cameras were recording the footage of the previous week on a regular basis every seven days. Security cameras were using VHS tapes in the early days. The tape's quality decreased as each recording lasted seven days in comparison to the previous week's. Caliente Sabroso was not the only business to fail to change security tapes on a regular basis. Managers confessed with a smile that he couldn't recall the last time the tapes were changed.

changed.

Every Wednesday, the employee of the supervisor utilized a forklift for lifting two pallets off a spot near the entrance to the warehouse. The location was hidden from surveillance cameras. No one ever inquired the reason. He was capable of navigating through the warehouse without a trace as he loaded the boxes on his truck without being seen by security cameras when they arrived. It was a sure-fire plan. They thought it was.

Rocky was amazed when I completed the report. Rocky informed me that an upgraded security system that had the ability to dim light as well as an alarm could have prevented the crime in a major way. Rocky was shaking his head when I finished my sentence. He stated, "The company doesn't want to spend this much money." Evidently the shrinkage was not a problem at $20,000.00. I looked at my shoulders and shrugged.

"You guys just lost 25 million dollars of stolen goods. It's the same issue. The problem will recur if do not make any adjustments."

Even though I didn't realise that at the time, my words were prophetic. It wouldn't be my last probe into unaccounted for inventory at Caliente Sabroso Foods.

The first time I worked as a private investigator was a huge success, and I started to build my abilities. Even though I didn't have any formal training, Mike was always available to help me learn about methods of investigation. I made mistakes, but determined to improve. When I fell short or injured when I was burned, I would conduct an after-action review. I would take a few minutes to think about my mistakes and offer suggestions to improve.

When I arrived at the surveillance site I would take a take a look at the map and try to find out how the subject might leave the location. It was quite surprising to me that this did not always occur in private investigations the way they do on TV. It is sometimes difficult to identify the subject, which is not so on television and in movies. I usually have descriptions of the subject, but it's not a photo. Sometimes, a physical description does not assist. One incident I'm aware of is of an white man who was twenty-four years old with a weight and height in proportion. I pulled up next to his home and saw five white males around 24 years old, get into five vehicles and drive in five directions. What was the right direction to to follow? It was a comedy of errors.

Sometimes, a physical description may be useful. My client was a black woman who was four feet tall, weighing 300 pounds. When she left the residence I was able be able to recognize her immediately. Surveillance is a job that relies on the physical description of the subject as well as the location of the address. To assist me in identifying the person, I examine the license plates of the vehicles that are present at the property.

The advent of social media makes it much easier. Everyone is eager to connect with others, share, like and even post. Social media search can often yield pictures of the subject, as well as details about their lives. One instance I can recall was when I viewed the page on Facebook of the person in question and discovered that she was part of the bowling club. After some digging I was able determine the date and time of the league's meeting. I was there the following night and had a great pizza and french fries. I captured video of her lifting and repeatedly bowling with a ball that weighs 12 pounds. It was impressive in the sense the fact that her injury was to her right hand and wrist the same hand and wrist she was using to bowl with. I was able to, after the night to move on to the next topic.

Surveillance is a laborious task that takes long hours of watching and waiting. Rarely do all appears to work. On a Saturday morning I pulled towards the home of my subject and turned off the motor. After eating breakfast tacos at Taco Cabana I spotted the large concrete mixer truck moving slowly towards me. The truck stopped just in the front of my subject's house and then moved on to his driveway. My subject.

Henry Graham walked out his front door wearing a long-sleeved, light blue cotton top, Levis and rubber work boots. Two guys with similar outfits were with Henry Graham. I quickly ripped the taco off and pulled out my camera.

The driver of the truck stepped out of the truck and returned to the rear of the truck where he controlled a number of hydraulic levers. Then he lower the chute, and then began pouring cement onto the area that was near to the driveway. Henry who was suffering from back pain, made the decision today to extend his driveway. I was able to record many videos. Henry spread the cement in an even manner across his new driveway with a bull flotation. Henry and his companions then kneeled down to apply the cement evenly on the driveway.

Fulmer Luck has struck again! It was extremely convenient to show up at Henry's home and find evidence that was incriminating within a matter of minutes. This was sadly the only instance, and not the norm. Surveillance is the act of watching and waiting. Sometimes, it may last for several hours. Sometimes for days. Private investigators tend to be more diligent than other investigators. To guarantee success we frequently rely on different techniques and tools.

Private investigators are most attracted by legal techniques.

Some people do not hesitate to look into illegal activities.

Chapter 6: Tricks Of Trade

It was a great option for cases like Cherry Jordan and Rosie Ramirez and Rosie Ramirez to use an ordinary-looking video camera. This was more than 20 years back. Since the time, technology for video cameras has advanced significantly. Modern covert cameras are roughly identical in dimensions to the size of a thumb drive. They can take vivid, high-definition color videos for long periods of time. These sophisticated covert cameras permit me to capture video from virtually any location. I can simply sit close to my subject in the bar or restaurant and record video without being aware. This is a major improvement over the first generation of covert cameras. The cameras were large and insecure and quickly depleted battery life.

The first of the cameras that I used as a covert camera was a wireless one that I tucked inside the San Antonio Spurs' logo-emblazoned drinking mug. I clipped the battery unit onto my belt, which was hidden under my shirt. It was large and heavy. The camera was unable to record video longer than 30 minutes. Its video signals are transmitted wirelessly through Bluetooth to a large and awkward receiver which I was able to carry on my belt. It was first utilized at a flea-market along Austin Highway in northeast San Antonio.

My client made herself jewelry and then sold it at a flea-market booth. The hand injury she suffered caused her to be in the workers' compensation system however she was able to spend the weekend selling her jewelry. I was able capture what I believed to be an excellent video of her with her hands, and working at her booth. After I left to review the video, it appeared that the quality was not great. A different electronic source frequently interfered with my wireless connection. My black-and-white footage was blurred because of the interruption. It became fuzzy after 10 seconds, just like the horizontal holds on an old black-and white TV. It was quite alarming. Magnum, P.I. has never witnessed this kind of thing.

To help me in my research, I began with equipment and other techniques. Every investigation is different. Sometimes you must think outside the box. The art, craft and technique of pretext can assist. This was a technique I acquired and perfected while working for Mike Farmer.

A pretext is in essence an unintentional phone call. It is possible to do this via through the telephone or even in person. This is when you call someone and claiming your identity in order to collect relevant information for your investigation. The use of pretexts is used by law enforcement officials as well as private investigators. It's basically undercover work. For instance, you could call the house of the suspect in a false pretense to see whether he or she actually is in the house. If the person you call responds then you've verified that information and can carry on surveillance. What happens if the spouse responds to the phone? In this scenario you simply portray you by stating that you are Bob Smith at XYZ Company. The spouse of the subject has been informed that you're conducting a job reference check on an employee who is new. Her husband is listed as a referee for the job. It's simple to locate all the details you need like his current location as well as his schedule of work and when he'll be at home. A specific program I used to change my telephone number was also accessible. It could make my new number appear on the caller ID, and every other phone number that I pick. This helps protect my identity. The use of pretexts is not legal in some states, such as California however I consider them an essential tools for investigation.

There are a variety of pretexts that are suitable for any situation. The one we used in the past wasn't illegal however it was not professional. It was because it encouraged the subject to engage in behavior they wouldn't normally be able to. After being monitored for a long time the method was employed when the subject was unable to leave the residence. Then, we would call an electric utility in the area informing them that we were present. We would inform them that there were sightings of an electric transformer that was in their street that was exploding and sparking. Then we asked politely whether the be willing to go outside and check whether the transformer was in good condition. We'd need to send a team to fix it if it was not. People are in love with helping others. They'll do it most often. When the subject left from the scene, we would take a seat in a car that was just a few homes below. The pretext was eventually dropped from one of our customers who inquired: "How come all your videos begin with the subject in front of their home , looking up at heaven?"

One of my initial pretexts was a man who could not leave his house. Following four consecutive days of not seeing any results I was waiting to see the results. The man was from Fredericksburg, Texas. I pretend to be an employee at our local store for groceries in order to call him. I congratulated him for winning our giveaway for groceries. He might be able to collect his voucher for groceries worth one hundred dollars in the next week? He was shocked by the opportunity. He was so elated that he could have put down his phone and then jumped in his car. I was just 1 mile away from him when he disappeared. I was only a mile away.

He smiled and ran into the supermarket as I was following his steps. When he left I was ready for an abrupt change in his attitude. It was the right thing to do. He left the place after a short time and didn't look at the surroundings. It's not an exaggeration to say the customer was unsatisfied. He was furious. Evidently, the supermarket didn't have any idea about the free one-hundred dollars grocery gift card. He continued to browse the store, searching for more details. He returned home, but has not returned to his house since. Although an insurance claim proved clear false, it has caused him pain.

Sometimes the pretext doesn't require a lot of effort. Sometimes, all it takes is a phone call. Jason Bell, a San Antonio man I wanted to meet was a construction worker but was not accessible. I was so upset that I started making calls to those who lived nearby, saying that he was supposed to sell me nice tires and rims. But I kept missing him. Two houses down, an elderly lady claimed that she had known Jason. He was building a parking lot for a convenience store near an intersection between Grissom Road & Tezel Road She said. I didn't ask her how she had figured it out. I hopped into my car for surveillance and headed towards the intersection.

After a few minutes I arrived at the convenience store only to see the construction team putting concrete in the parking area. Seven workers were present. There were seven employees. There were two who were Hispanic Five other males were white. All of them were dressed in the same fashion. However, I didn't have a picture of Jason. I didn't have any pictures of Jason. As I became stressed, I thought of Jason's phone number. I quickly positioned my car in a position where the construction workers could observe it. I reached out with my left hand and grabbed my camera and began to record. I utilized the left side of my hand to dial Jason's phone number. The crew was also watching me. One of the crew members took out a cellphone from his pocket. The phone was ringing. Jason telling Jason "hello" on the other side. I smiled, then swiftly put down the phone. While Jason was working I continued to shoot footage. He put his cellphone in his pocket, and continued. The next couple of hours I was able to film a stunning footage of Jason spreading asphalt across the parking lot that was newly constructed.

The pretext could be useful as an investigative tool. However, there are a few limitations. You cannot claim to be police officers or clergy. It is not a way to collect financial information. I will not make any reason to oblige the subject to perform an unintended manner of behavior. It's not difficult to entice the subject once you've taken this method. Roping happens when a private investigator sets up an environment that forces the subject to engage in some type of physical action. The investigator captures the action on video. We didn't use any excuse to request the subject to leave in order to be able to determine their identity. They wouldn't walk outside unless they had been seriously injured.

Private investigators can rope an individual to public places such as an outlet mall or a cinema. Once the person has got out of his car and left, the investigator is going to blow up one tire. The private investigator will force the driver to change his tire after returning to find that the tire is flat. All of this is documented and analyzed by the police. Although it's a violation of the law however, it's not unusual private investigators do this. They carry small, metal tire valves that inflate tires. My excuses are soliciting information or asking for their names.

I once accompanied a woman, who I assumed was the subject from her house to the supermarket. The person in question was a white woman of thirty-something with long blonde hair. She was about five eight inches tall and appeared to smile quite often. The woman she was with was a woman who also matched with the characteristics of my subject. However, I was certain that the lady I was talking to was my subject, I wanted to verify. To determine her identity I followed her to the supermarket. I quickly grabbed a grocery bag. I added several things to look like I was in the store. Then I approached slowly while she walked along one of the aisles. Once I attracted her attention and she made a gesture towards me. I responded, "Hello...I know you." I was staring at her in a blank stare and was able to understand. I responded, "I believe we went to the identical high school." I looked at her with a frown when she tried to find my name in the name. I askedher "What's the name of yours? ".

She said, "Rachel." Bingo. The subject was her. I changed my mind quickly.

"Oh, wow. "I was thinking you were Tina Dockery," he continued. "I was there."

Clark High School together. You're exactly like her." She said something , and we separated. I rushed back to the car, and then waited on my companion to get out. Normally, I don't allow a person to be able to see my face. In this case I had no other choice. This was the only method I could pinpoint the issue.

Sometimes, pretexts are needed in situations where there isn't enough information available.

This brings me back to the mystery of the unnamed golfer.

One person once stated that the best thing to do "...to golf be to spoil a enjoyable walk." I'm not sure if this is the case. However, I know when you're getting workers' comp because of injuries to your back while at work, and also playing golf, the fairway may be unfair. Fernando Sosa was one such instance.

Like numerous investigations, I didn't know the exact location where Fernando resided. Even though there were two addresses for him, both were old. The mail was delivered to a postbox this is an old technique employed to defraud professional. I wasn't aware of the kind of car he was driving. To be truthful, I did not know anything regarding his name. Sosa. The ability to see through the hardboiled private investigator is a legend. Sometimes it is due to a lack of communication between the claims adjuster and the private investigator. The majority of claims are too overwhelming for the claims handlers. Sometimes they do not provide investigators all the data they possess.

Fernando's claims are an illustration of this. I took out my laptop and began to log into the database that is proprietary which is another tool I use to conduct my research.

While we appreciate the Sandra Bullock Film, The Net, and Kiefer's television show 24 for their work There isn't a single databases that private detectives have the ability to access to reveal the whole story. The only thing you can do is gather pieces. Investigators who are private have access exclusive databases that aren't accessible to the general public. The databases include information gleaned from credit heads[37, utility records, as well as rental application, in addition to other private and public sources. I can also examine license plates and VIN numbers, and conduct titles checks on personal as well as commercial watercraft, aircraft as well as commercial vehicles. The databases can be used as a tool used by experienced private investigators. You may be amazed at the amount of public information and social media sites that private investigators can use. A lot of the information contained in databases must be checked through private investigators with shoes leather. You can also wander through the streets and approach doors to ask questions. This is how I came across Fernando's home located on Leopard Street in Corpus Christi Texas.

Corpus Christi, a South Texas city, was founded in 1839, as Kinney's Trading Post. It is the "Sparkling city in the middle of the ocean" is a popular tourist destination and the eighth-largest cities in Texas. The downtown area is situated on the Western Gulf of Mexico, close to Corpus Christi Bay. This is the 8th largest port within the United States. Lexington is was an Essex Class aircraft carrier that was used during the Pacific during World War Two. The nearby Padre Island National Sea Shore The longest barrier undeveloped island anywhere in the globe is a favorite beach destination for millions of people.

Fernando was my target for surveillance But I didn't get any evidence over the course of two days. I've never met anyone that matched his description. There were numerous vehicles parked around the residence. I checked the plates on every vehicle but they all was registered as belonging to the owner of the property. It was discovered that they were registered to addresses I'd not heard of, and with names I had never heard of. It put me in the mood of a bad person. In addition I was able to see the neighbor from her kitchen window to my surveillance vehicle. It was just a matter of time before the police showed up. I asked them about what I was doing in the area. It was like a flash of change.

Two Hispanic men strolled up the front door, and began an exchange. Based on their estimated weights and ages the one could easily been Fernando. My private investigation didn't succeed however I was always convinced that I could still be able to get an assignment to determine the weight and the age of performers in circus. From having just one suspect to having two was capable of having them all. Lektion 42: Take video whenever you are in doubt. It's better to take video only to discover later that the video wasn't taken by you, rather as opposed to not capture video only to later discover the truth. I took video.

Two men were in the parking lot talking, and then an 18-year-old came in carrying two golf carts. The sight of bags forced me to sit up straight inside my vehicle. This could make sense I thought. The teenager threw the bags in the trunk of the Chevrolet Lumina in pale blue and the two men dispersed. The first man went back to his house while the second driver drove the Chevy along with the teenager. They both pulled off their driveways and started to drive through the streets. I paused for a moment. Should I follow contestant 1 , at home? Or do I follow the contestant number 2. In my more than 30 years of private investigation I've had to make quick choices based on less than full information numerous times. Regarding the first man I was able to go back to my home and start again. In light of the info found in those golf bags I determined that following contestant 2. was the best choice. It is more beneficial to follow contestant 2 and eventually eliminate him as the person in question rather than letting him go, only to realize later that the contestant was.

It was a great experience. Chevy served as my driver for the duration of 30 minutes. It felt like a long time, but it was really just a an issue of duration. Then we finally arrived at Oso Beach Municipal Golf Course, South Alameda Street. When I walked alongside him into his parking area I felt a rush of adrenaline. Fernando is believed to suffer from an injury to the back. The video could have been great film should it turn out as Fernando.

I quickly moved into position and captured video footage of him pulling off one of the bags belonging to him from his trunk, and threw the bag onto his back. The teenager and he took off for our course. He wasn't my course therefore I had to find the individual. It happens from time every now and then. Customers aren't always aware when you record footage of the wrong individual. It's important to determine the person as quickly as you can during surveillance. I wanted to know whether this was Fernando. While Fernando as well as "little

Fernando," carried their clubs, as well as an emerald mesh bucket containing the white balls of golf, I was stunned.

When his identification as Fernando I decided to record an instant video of Fernando at the drive-way. Because I was able to meet him and discover that I was his subject I couldn't bear to stand for him. My presence could be considered unsettling. There was an outdoor bench just behind him on his shooting area. I was able capture approximately 30 minutes of footage. He was wearing a pair of plaid pants that were sloppy, bent over, and put an unassuming Titleist golf club on the golf tee. Then he stood and dragged his golf club to the left. Then he swung it up and down until he heard you heard the usual sound came from the golf club hitting the ball. The ball soared through the air, and was almost beyond my reach. A golf ball that is hit with back injuries is the most dangerous thing you could do. The whole thing is about twisting, and bent the back.

After about 30 minutes of footage I decided to take the time to put down my secret camera. I approached the man and began a pretext. It was quite simple. It was easy. I asked him his name.

"Excuse me I'm sorry, but do you identify yourself as Fernando Sosa?" He asked. He looked at me , then changed his gaze. This was the moment to be honest.

He replied, "Yeah." "What's up?"

It was he who actually did it. He was the one who did it. I'm not sure how I could have responded had I had asked him to not. I said, "I was just at the pro shop, and there's a phone call to you." "I believe it's crucial." It was a long time prior to the time that cellphones were commonplace. I thanked him and then he gave the golf club to Fernando. As he was about depart, I could hear him take off the Velcro securer from his leather golf glove. He then began heading towards the proshop. I swiftly made a U-turn and walked out as swiftly as I could. I then spent the remainder of the day recording more footage of him inside my surveillance vehicle that was parked in the parking lot. As per his medical records,

Fernando Sosa was an extremely rare and delicate flower. He was not observed on the driving range by a renowned doctor. He was a formidable golfer.

Fernando Sosa's story isn't common. In reality insurers need to be aware of the numerous indicators that could suggest fraud. According to one source those who are injured playing on weekends typically return to work on Mondays , and blame the injury on their job. This is to claim workers' compensation payments for an injury that isn't directly related to work. The red flags are an additional instrument used by investigators as well as adjusters of claims to identify fraud.

Private investigators also utilize GPS trackers in addition to hidden cameras as well as databases and pretexts. GPS (or Global Positioning System trackers) are tiny devices about similar to an ordinary pager. They transmit an electronic signal each second to the cell phone network or satellite orbiting Earth. The signal is transmitted back to a website which may interface with a map. My surveillance vehicle is equipped with the tablet computer on top. I monitor your vehicle's movements from A to B by using maps. I can determine the time when your car was in motion or if it was idle. I can also track the speed at which you drive. If you are lost in the traffic, I will easily use my tracking software to quickly find your destination.

I have high-end, commercial-grade GPS trackers. I keep them in sturdy plastic, waterproof pelican containers. The magnet connects to the underside of the car using the weight of 90 pounds. It's not as straightforward as it appears on television. There are places where signals cannot be detected. Automobile makers are now making large use of plastic and rubber in their newer models. It can be difficult at times to locate the right place for the tracker to be attached. It is essential to charge the GPS tracker battery frequently. The special extended 30-day batteries are what I have in mind so that I don't need to replace the device more frequently than once every month. The subject didn't wash her car, and I've misplaced one of my trackers.

It was a horrible divorce trial in Grand Junction Colorado. Stella Kaufmann, the soon-to-be ex-wife of the client put an GPS tracker beneath the Blue Lincoln Navigator. The initial few weeks were a good beginning. She carried on her usual business doing errands and was with her lover on Fridays and Tuesdays to have afternoon tea in a motel near to where the junction between Interstate Highway 70 and Horizon Drive. Everything was going well when the light stopped a commercial park, and stood still for the whole weekend. The signal disappeared on the next morning. Initial thoughts were that the battery was failing. After some investigation I realized that Stella's lawyer was the final address for my missing-in action tracker.

Trent Kaufmann, my client I was informed later by him that his ex-wife had contacted him and accused him of place a tracker inside her car in the hope to stalk her. Stella was able trust the man and inform him that he had not put the tracker inside her car. Evidently she was committed to maintaining her car in good condition. This GPS device was located inside a small pelican-shaped, black, case which she took to a car wash that was self-service. While she was not knowledgeable about cars and the device was a bit odd to her, she went straight to her attorney and was recognized by the device instantly. GPS trackers have proved invaluable in finding and monitoring the situation in every other case. But I was sad to lose the $300,000 GPS tracker.

Private eyes employ equipment like GPS trackers, as well as other tools in their trade and what you watch on television and in films can be inaccurate. While private investigators might employ a variety of tools however, our primary tools are camera, phone and computers.

From 1998 to 1998, I was a police officer as a judicial intern for Mike Farmer. Then, in August of 1998 I was awarded the Master of Arts in Criminal Justice degree from UTSA. With a college education I began looking at other career options. While I did learn much through

Mike Farmer, I didn't think of it as a career that could last for an entire lifetime. There weren't any benefits or actual opportunities to grow and I was unable to make the most of the numerous opportunities. Furthermore, I was also mom to three kids who had disabled and one was less than five . Also, I had a large amount in student loans which meant it wasn't the best time to become an investigator by myself. I wanted a reliable solution that would be beneficial to my family, as well as increase my skills as an investigator. It was available through a federal contractor. I was given U.S. Government credentials as along with an identification badge. In the beginning, I had be taken to Pennsylvania to be instructed by officials in underground caves.

Chapter 7: George Bus And The Secret Government Cavern

I felt like Batman. After receiving the top-secret security clearance granted by authorities of the U.S. government I was allowed to begin my underground training, located 230 feet beneath the surface in a cave situated in the countryside of Pennsylvania. The government facility was protected and was manned by security guards equipped with guns that were automatic. This isn't Robert Ludlum's first scene. This was the real me in January 1999.

My father informed me of the company known as US in the summer of 1998.

Investigations Services was looking for employees. It was a brand new company to me. I visited the San Antonio office in a three-story structure, close to Broadway along Loop 410 to fill out an application. I was stunned to learn that the person who took my application came from Chicago. I immediately jumped into Carl Sandburg's famous poem Chicago "...Stormy in addition to the raucous city of Big Shoulders

39[. She was enthralled, and I watched her as she put my application at the top of the pile. It isn't important how much it will cost I guess.

US Investigations Services was established in 1996 following that the U.S. Office of Personnel Management (OPM) and its investigatory arm, OFI (Office for Federal Investigations(OFI) was privatized. This was in part because of Al Gore, then Vice President,'s efforts in reducing the bureaucracy and regulation of government. Up until this point, OFI was responsible to manage the bulk of background investigation of government candidates and periodically reconsultations for employees of the government who had security clearances. Each five-year period, holders of security clearances will be re-examined to ensure they're still eligible for clearance. US Investigations Services was privatized and became an employee-owned firm which conducted about two-thirds (or greater) of the background investigations conducted by OPM.

USIS required six months in order to finish their background check. Then, I realized that they'd lost my application. The average processing time for USIS is not more than 3 weeks. It was interesting to observe that their negligence with my documents would result in tragic events in the years following. At present, however I was employed. I was hired. U.S. government granted me an extremely secure security clearance, and told me to travel into Butler in Pennsylvania to begin my education.

Mike Farmer was informed by me that I was moving ahead. I was concerned regarding his reactions. Excellent investigators are hard to come across in this competitive field of insurance claims surveillance. My worries turned out to not be true as he dealt with the situation very effectively. He was extremely kind and generous. He was extremely excited regarding me and my potential. He provided me with some weeks of severance and wished me success on my new business ventures. He also said that he was expecting to receive the same from me when I had graduated from college. It was a blessing that we ended our relationship on reasonable terms. Mike Farmer would be my final job. In actual fact, Mike gave an interview several years later to the reporter of The MidMissouri Business Journal. I was interview by the journalist. Mike described me as one of the most competent investigators he'd ever met. This pretty much is the whole point.

After the Christmas season, I boarded an airplane to Cleveland and emerged from Cleveland Hopkins International Airport in the coldest winter I've ever experienced. The cold breeze from Lake Erie was a chilling force against my face. I was afraid I'd be frozen to death. I took the airport shuttle to the car rental place which I quickly got into a warm rental vehicle before accelerating down the highway toward Butler.

Butler is a tiny community with a population of around 13,000, is located just a little over thirty miles north of Pittsburgh. It is situated in the countryside of Pennsylvania with breathtaking panoramas over Christmas trees as well as dense forests. The course was three weeks in duration. I stayed each night in the Marriott Hotel, Butler, along with fellow trainees. Every morning I drove 18 miles to the north, which took me to a secret government facility situated near west of Annandale. When I arrived within Annandale (which was in essence the location of a general store and a post office) I then took Branchton Road to my left. It's a country road that runs through dense forests at both ends. About a mile further along on the highway, I reached an abrupt bend, that I noticed something unique. A huge clearing to the right of the highway had numerous parking areas which were completely filled with vehicles. There was no structure to be seen. It was revealed that the official instruction I received was several hundred feet below the ground in the cave. They refused to let me in when I arrived at first.

This cave is an older limestone mine which government of the U.S. government purchased in 1958.

For the storage of government documents. Underground climate is managed naturally and temperatures stay constant all year. Cool temperatures and low humidity helps keep government documents in good condition. They're big enough to allow semi-trailers to move side by side. The walls are all made of whitewashed, solid limestone. The storefront could be described as one every couple of yards. OPM or USIS were clearly labeled. Some were not. There were records reportedly that were stored in the mine by several U.S. intelligence agencies. There is a belief that this mine could stand up to direct nuclear attacks. This is another reason that records are maintained in the mining facility for the use of government. It wasn't something I needed to know.

OPM as well as USIS have offices in the mine. [42] I pulled up my car and began walking through the long, blue-tinted path from the parking lot towards the entrance to the mine. Two separate entrances to security were open with uniformed and security personnel armed who verified every person's identity, and carried automatic weapons. I was advised I was required to go into the cave for instruction. Security did not have any evidence of me being part of the course. Security guards made several phone calls, and I sat there for a total of twenty minutes. The problem was eventually completed. I went into the cave and went right. After walking for a hundred metres until the USIS storefront, I walked through the door to my new job.

Initial training was focused around the USIS history and how wonderful they were. The majority of the instruction included OPM procedures along with government processes as well as extensive training for conducting interviews and taking statements. Following three months of training I hopped on an airplane in Cleveland and took a flight into Dallas, Texas, where I began working for USIS at the Dallas District Office. The office was situated in Commerce Street, on the eighth floor of the Earle Cabell Federal Building. The video intercom permitted access into the office. Gavin Kingston, USIS secretary could see me standing in the corridor , when I activated the intercom. The button was hit to unlock the door lock that was powered by electricity. When I heard the loud buzzer I moved on the lever to allow access. Gavin was an old male, slightly overweight sporting long hair of white. Gavin was approaching his late sixties and was close to retiring after working for nearly thirty years at OPM as well as USIS.

Bill Moss, a senior trainer I was my instructor for the first two or three weeks. Prior to the privatization process and the creation of USIS He had been employed in the federal field as an investigator with OFI. Moss was just shorter than six feet, and was brown with eyes that were green. He appeared to see all things. He was an absolute professional and, despite his quiet demeanour I was well-trained by him. Then, after lunch, I went back into the building that was that was locked down. This building wasn't permitted to be accessed by police. Numerous police cars belonging FPS, the Federal Protective Service(FPS)[43were discovered in odd positions close to the building's entry point. It appeared as if they arrived in a rush. The building was home to the Internal Revenue Service (IRS) that had a branch office within this same location. Someone left a notepad bag outside of their office. While the police were preparing to summon the bomb squad, a brave person was able to look inside and saw the lunch bag of an employee.

OPM offered me an laptop computer that was encrypted for my work in investigation. It was referred to as"GRiD. "GRiD." Even though it was not the most technologically advanced the computer weighed at a ton and was virtually impervious to destruction. This was the time in my course when I first heard about the incident that has been told repeatedly that it has been made into OPM legend. The story was about a government investigator who had his car damaged and smashed into. The investigator's GRiD laptop was one of the stolen items. The police later discovered their GRiD laptop laptop inside a nearby trash bin. Evidently, the person who stole it believed that it was garbage. It was funny and something that my fellow investigators and I could all understand. The

GRiD computers were eventually replaced by brand new Compass Presario laptops.

After I completed my course under Bill Moss, I spent most times in Ft. Worth and Arlington working for officials from the Immigration and Naturalization Service, Federal Bureau of Prisons, U.S. Attorney's Office, as well as other personnel at federal and state agencies. Every every day brought a new adventure.

Once I was interviewing the regional director of the INS in the Dallas office. But I was not able to remain in my chair. The office he worked in was the most expensive Brown leather seats. I was beginning to fall off the chair while I sat down and talked to him. I could not remain on the chair no matter how hard I tried. He did not even speak to me in case the director noticed. He was very friendly to me.

After he'd moved on to his topic the conversation turned to about his recent trip. He was sat in the chair, droning on, and I was forced put my footwear on floor and secure my knees to ensure I could remain on the seat. I left, in awe of why the government would spend the money to purchase leather furniture. Maybe it was due to the fact that they did not have to interview the INS regional director didn't need to sit through lengthy interviews.

The people I spoke to were as warm like the INS director. Boone was a man of a younger age who I did background checks on. He was a candidate for a position with the U.S. He had applied for a job in the U.S. Marshal Service. Roy Booker, his uncle was named as a reference. Roy was an deputy U.S. Marshal. Roy was an Assistant U.S. Marshall in Ft. Worth, Texas. Evidently, Boone was following in the footsteps of his uncle. To schedule the appointment I dialed the number, and it was discovered that Roy called from home. I had a brief conversation with his wife. I left her a voicemail and she was extremely nice. Roy Booker called me shortly after. It was an incredible opportunity to meet an U.S. Marshal. Marshal. Roy began to mock me calling his home phone to talk to his wife. Then I told him who I was and why it was meant for Boone the nephew of Boone. He didn't care. He was adamant about me from every angle. He advised me to try something that was physically impossible and I gave up.

Following six months work at USIS in Dallas, Wanda Ashworth, the Dallas District Manager of USIS I was contacted by Wanda Ashworth, the Dallas District Manager for USIS. Wanda Ashworth, a fellow Texasan worked for OFI for a long time prior to becoming a part of USIS. In her 60s, she was beautiful with long brown hair with a warm smile. She asked me whether I was considering moving. She was just opening an office for one person located in Huntsville, Texas. She believed that I was the ideal person to run the station. Even though I wasn't thrilled to move , I was keen to be a successful and flexible worker in my new job. We packed everything up and relocated from Huntsville, Texas, despite the recent relocation to San Antonio, Texas to Arlington, Texas.

Huntsville, Texas is home to 38,000 residents. It's located in the piney forests in East Texas. It's situated midway the distance between Houston as well as Dallas in Interstate 45. Huntsville is home to TDCJ, the Texas Department of Criminal Justice, (TDCJ), and there are around 10 state prisons within. Sam Houston State University is located in Huntsville. We rented a spacious 2-story house on Avenues. I was back in Federal security investigations into background checks. Because Huntsville as my current home base I travelled across eastern Texas to investigate different universities and colleges which included Texas A&M University (TX), Stephen F. Austin University (Sam Houston State University) and Blinn college. My work was in large part connected to the BOP and I was able to spend a significant amount of time in Huntsville as well as Texas the state jails. I also participated in a variety of investigations at the National Aeronautics and Space Administration (NASA)[45[45 Lyndon B. Johnson Space Center, Houston. NASA as well as Ft. Worth were the most secure facilities I've ever witnessed or encountered in regards to security.

One of my first significant assignments was to conduct background checks in the national security field for the employees in the George H. W. Bush Presidential Library and Museum. It is located in College Station, Texas. Bush Library is located in Research Park, on the west campus of Texas A&M University in College Station. It was built with a price of $43 million The property is spread over 90 acres. It houses the presidential library, museum and two auditoriums, as well as the Annenberg Presidential Conference Center, and the George Bush School of Government and Public Service. A tiny space on the 2nd floor of the building is the place where the president Bush as well as Bush's wife. Bush live when they visit. I had the opportunity to visit the museum as I was conducting my research. Being a veteran of the war I discovered that the Gulf War exhibit very interesting. Collections of the presidential administration from George H. W. Bush (41st president of the United States) is housed in the library. It has more than 44 million documents, papers as well as two million photos. Additionally, there are hundreds of videos and artifacts. The Presidential Libraries Act of 1955

[46] and National Archives and Records Administration(NARA)[47] govern the library.

The Bush Library, which had opened for less than two years ago, was in flux at the time I joined. I conducted background research on Spencer Winthrop (the new director of the Bush Library), as and numerous NARA Archivists. It was 1999, one of the most difficult year of Bill Clinton's presidency. A large portion of the NARA Archivists who were later to relocate from Little Rock, Arkansas to work at the Clinton Presidential Library were in their training at the Bush Library. The majority of their periodic review was conducted by me.

NARA was the manager of the library and the museum However, there was an atmosphere of political sway. There was lots of pressure on me, and I had high hopes for the outcomes of my research. While it was something I was feeling, I did not allow myself to be influenced by it. These types of games aren't something I've ever played. Wanda Ashworth, who was conducting the interview to have Winthrop's security clearance granted and casually reminded me of Winthrop's status as government employee working for NARA. But, he was an intimate friend of the Bush family and therefore was essentially selected to become the new director of the library and museum. After that, she paused in her tracks and allowed the message to hang into the sky for a few minutes. Her message was simple, and I understood the message. This meant I had adhere to the law and be able to exercise discretion when conducting my investigation. I followed this procedure for each investigation, no matter what the nature of the investigation.

Winthrop was extremely friendly and easy to collaborate with. Prior to the interview the interview, he greeted me in his office and handed me ice cold Dr. Pepper. He wasn't trying to get us to do something I would like to believe. He was an Southern Methodist University graduate and just wanted to discuss their football game with arch-rivals, TCU Horned Frogs. TCU Horned Frogs. A large portion of the librarians in the library were SMU alumni, and they were close friends too. They were referred to as Smoothies as well as the SMU Mafia by museum staff. They planned to meet to have a barbeque prior to playing in the biggest game.

Steve Redd, a childhood friend who was working on his Ph.D. at the George Bush School of Government and Public Service. While I visited, we frequently had lunch together. I and he could attend the C-SPAN[48] event that was broadcast from the auditorium located at Bush Library. Bush Library. It was President Bush spoke briefly, but leaving early. This was my first encounter with an U.S. the President. Bush was larger than he did on television. It appeared like there was a lot of people standing and cheering. If the president Bush had coughed I'm certain that all of us would have stood to applaud. Additionally, I was given the privilege to meet Leon Panetta [49Former chief of staff member of the president Bill Clinton and future CIA Director under Barack Obama. There was also Senator John Kasich as well as Senator John Kasich, the Ohio U.S. Representative and the chairman of The

House Budget Committee. Kasich will be a presidential candidate in the United States in 2016. I'd be spending much of my time in Texas A&M doing investigations. A lot of them required security clearances given to me by the U.S. Department of Energy.

A tiny, one megawatt research reactor is situated in a wooded area , near Bush Presidential Library. Bush Presidential Library. College Station residents don't know that a nuclear plant is within their backyard. It's part of Texas A&M's nuclear engineering department which is used to educate students and also making radioactive isotopes that are used in study. It is located close to Easterwood Airport, on the Nuclear Science Road. The year 2000 was the time I became the responsible for all background investigations for national security within the nuclear engineering department. This included students and faculty. Due to their work being classified some faculty members were granted an Q clearance from the DOE. There are particular guidelines to conduct federal background checks, based of whether an investigation has been regular or new investigation that is re-instigated. The blue OPM binder I carried with me everywhere I wrote down the number of sources or sources must be questioned. Sources must address specific periods during the course of the subject's life. It is crucial to discuss any gap in time between work and school. Sometimes it's hard to locate sources like Roy Phillips who was applying for an AQ clearance. Roxanne was Roy's girlfriend. She was the only one who was able to talk about a short period of self-employment he was working prior to his time at Texas A&M. She was there at the time Roy was detained at Dixie Chicken in Bryan, Texas and charged with public intoxication.

Roy and his girlfriend resided in a shabby apartment near the campus during the day of interviews. Roy was native to Stephenville Texas, had just finished his nuclear engineering degree and had applied for a job with the DOE. I visited Roy at the door of his apartment and he offered me a firm handshake which could remove the rust from the doorknob. Roy was not an undergraduate student studying nuclear engineering. The tall man was muscular and wore a western t-shirt with a buttoned shirt along with faded and soiled Levi's. He was quiet and reserved and his answers were punctuated by "yes sir" and "no sir". He sounded a lot as that of the Marlboro Man. Roxanne was quite the opposite. She was a petite pretty blonde girl wearing a baby blue tank top which just barely covered her breasts, paired with the beige mini skirt. Additionally, she didn't appear to be wearing a bra. This was an incident I did not think about. It was the month of May it was May, College Station was already hot and humid. The whole thing made sense following the events that were to follow. Normally I would be interviewing Roy first. Since Roxanne was at the scene of the arrest of public intoxication I decided to speak with Roxanne first. I wanted to get her perspective before I inquired about Roy what he thought of his. Roy was able to excuse himself while he walked slowly up the stairs, which are carpeted and leads towards their 2nd floor home. Roxanne moved for me to take an armchair at the foot of the couch. After Roy's footsteps had slowed down I could hear creaking of the stairs. Roxanne was given my official documents after I heard the door to the upstairs open. To my left, she sat down on the sofa. When she did this she noticed that the skirt's hemline grew to mid-thigh level, showing the firm thighs and brown legs.

It is crucial to build the trust of your subject when interviewing them. It is best to begin with having fun, and then save the more crucial questions for later. It is crucial to make your subject feel at ease with you and be able to trust you in order to ensure they are honest and honest in their responses. Roxanne appeared like she was trying to build trust with me in this particular instance. She lean forward during the interview, which allowed me to look at her extensive decolletage. She smiled a lot. Maybe a bit too often. Each when I made a joke she laughed a bit too loudly and too long. She even put her hands on my knees. Roxanne appeared to try to influence the investigation, which I thought. Investigators employ"steering" to describe someone who tries "steering" to refer to those who attempt to direct an investigation in their favor.

Roxanne was I asked during the course of my interview whether Roy has ever been in contact with foreigners. Roxanne laughed and then threw her head back, as in case she was not convinced by the question. "No. "No, sir!" She stopped for a moment and then glanced to me in a sly glance. She turned her head and shook it to reveal her long dark, long, and dark eyelashes. I wasn't expecting her to be doing something, but she stared at me. She swung her legs and showed that she did not have underwear.

It was certainly a first. It was something she had never done before.

It was astonishing. It was quite shocking to observe. It was clear that she didn't have bras because she was humid and hot in Texas. I murmured, "Uh!" It took me some time to figure out the words. "Uh, no. "This is not an interview." She was able to remind me. This is an inquiry to get a security clearance from the government. Roy ..." Roy most effective option is assist her. I stopped, pointed at her, then I tapped my finger to ask her to close her legs. "... Answer every question honestly.

It's not clear what she was feeling, if she was scared or both. She took a long look at me before snapping her legs closed so fast that I believed I heard bony cartilage crackle. The conversation was ended in a cold silence. Her smile, cheerful and relaxed attitude quickly vanished. I went through the interview fast followed by an interview with Roy and then left the room. In the Texas heat, I recall walking back to my car, saying "It's amazing!"

Wanda was not surprised to learn that I had written about this incident earlier in the day. She was curious to be aware of whether Roy was the one who made Roxanne to the blame. This was a serious accusation. Based upon the conversations I had with Roy nevertheless, it seemed evident that he was only in business. Roy offered me numerous sources. I also created my own. They all proved his status as a tough man. Wanda wanted to know if I was sure. He didn't like it. The girl was only 18 years old. She was young and undeveloped and most likely believed it was her way of helping her boyfriend. Wanda told me to keep a record of the entire event as it occurred and to notify Roxanne be aware if she reached out to me with any reason. The job was expected to be interesting and that's the main thing.

Chapter 8: Dying With Your Eyes Open

Bernard Kerik, former New York City Police Commissioner once stated"that "Going to prison is as if you're dying without your eyes shut." I witnessed this in the exhausted eyes of the inmates in the prisons I visited, as well in the eyes of a few correctional officers that looked after the inmates. Kerik could relate. After a distinguished time with his New York City Police Department He was sentenced to 4 years of federal jail for fraud.

While working for USIS I was able to spend most times in different prisons both in the state and federal. FMC Carswell was the first Federal prison I visited. It is a home for women suffering from medical and mental health problems. It is located on grounds of the Fort Worth Naval Air Station Joint Readiness Base (JRB) [55] located on the west side of Ft. Worth. Lynette "Squeaky" was one of the Manson Family member who tried to assassinate President Gerald R. Ford, was held in the 1990s. FMC Carswell was also the first time I came across the BOP. The BOP was an integral part of several of my background investigations. A majority of them involved regular reinvestigation and re-inspection of correctional officers in the current system and other staff members of the government.

It was surreal to walk into the prison grounds once I passed Security for the very first time. Once I had parked my car, I went into to the main reception room. Two federal correctional officers in uniform dressed in white shirts with starched sleeves and navy blue pants were seated inside, looking over a massive security console. There were several security monitors that were flickering on the walls as well as an array of black Motorola two-way radios, which were held by hands and stored inside their charging cases. There were several keys in large brass were also discovered at the back of the room. The federal IDs of my client were placed by the glass. He then began pressing a huge blue button in his computer. I moved my head to my left watching as the massive steel-encased electric door slowly opened. I walked through the door and was welcomed by a tiny space that was five feet in size. It was situated between two sets of doors that were secured. The first door closing slowly until I heard the metallic "thunk". This door had been locked, and I couldn't open it until someone opened it again. After closing the glass and steel doors I was waiting for the next to be opened. Both doors could not be closed at the same time in order to safeguard the security of the others. Then, I entered the second entrance onto the grounds of the prison. It wasn't what I was expecting however, it was reminiscent of a tiny Junior college.

I spent the majority part of the time in Huntsville going to the various Texas federal prisons. In the case of Huntsville, Huntsville Unit was the first. It was established in 1849, prior to it was destroyed by the Civil War. It was Texas the nation's first penitentiary. The 15-foot red brick walls which surround it today are known as The Walls. The Walls were home to soldiers during The Civil War, it was the home of Union soldiers who were captured during the Civil War. It's located on an area of around four acres, and is located just two blocks from the town square. The past guests included John Wesley Hardin (Old West outlaw gunfighter),[57] Hawaiian bounty hunter, and reality television celebrity Duane

Chapman [58Chapman [58]] and Texas drug Kingpin Fred are known as "Dog The Bounty Hunter".

Carrasco[59], just to name only a handful of.

As I walked in The Walls' front door I was able to smell disinfectant. It was a scent I soon grew accustomed to. Every one of the Texas state prisons utilized identical disinfectants. I walked into the air-conditioned administrative offices in the front and then through two distinct security doors. The hallway that ran throughout the office was narrow and long. There were two massive holding cells located at the opposite end of the hallway. Two benches ran along the length of each of the two cells that were held. They were used to temporarily keep inmates in place when they were on journey to the court or transferred to a state prison. The work of art made by prisoners over time was displayed on the walls that separated the huge cells. The quality and talent of the art work amazed me. The majority of the artworks are to museums. It was evident in my mind that this amazing talent was not yet reaching its divine potential.

The Texas deathhouse is located within the Walls. This is the Allan B. Polunsky Unit is situated near Livingston, Texas, and is just a half hour away from the death row. I'd been to the prison several times in the past and did not want to go back. Death row inmates reside in the building number twelve. They are dressed in the same prison clothing like all Texas prisoners. Their prison clothes feature an enormous black "DR" that is printed in block letters on the back.

Sergeant Sam Cook was back at the Walls when I saw him. Hair was blonde and slender and he looked similar to Jim Gaffigan. He was jovial, despite the job and had a good attitude. He was uniformed in the same way like all state correctional officers. They quickly became close acquaintances. Sam was an TDCJ trainer for several years. Sam was in a position to meet numerous state correctional officers who been pursuing BOP jobs. The federal government seems to pay correctional officers more and offer more benefits. Sam was acquainted with the officers, which allowed me to to use Sam to conduct background checks.

Some Texas correctional officers I met were helpful or kind. I once had the opportunity to go to Lovelady, Texas to interview TDCJ's Eastham Unit warden. Clyde Barrow, also known as "The Ham" by inmates who were held there, was once detained. Clyde became free in 1932. He travelled to Dallas where he came across Bonnie Parker. Bonnie and Clyde were to be reunited two years later on the lonely road that ran through Louisiana. They were slain and attacked at the hands Frank Hamer, a legendary Texas Ranger along with 4 other Texas law enforcement officials.

At the time of my arrival I presented my federal identification at the entrance. After that, I was brought to the warden's office. When I arrived the warden Buford Ellis had warned me. He was known as a TDCJ member due to his inability to deal with and could be very irritable. He was the Warden of one of the most challenging prisons for prisoners of state in the United States and was appreciated because of his capability to maintain things in order. Violet the secretary of his requested an appointment. I knew that this was going to be a challenge. I wasn't a regular participant. This was contrary to the procedure of investigating. To surprise people I spoke with I needed to make sure that they didn't get taken by surprise and didn't need to write their own statements. Warden Ellis was not thrilled about the situation. He was short, sporting gray buzz cut and a reddish-colored face. The old suit was small for him, and his voice was very deep. I wanted to inform him that the 1970's were the decade that called and wanted to return their suits but I wasn't certain it would be helpful to my situation. The truth was that it would not have made a difference. I did not ask him to be interviewed. I informed him that I did an investigation of national security background checks on an old TDCJ

Captain who was applying for an BOP job. I could have explained to Ellis about my sales of Sports Illustrated subscriptions. Ellis did not seem to notice. He almost didn't even notice me. He said, "I'm no giving a statement" before leaving his office, left me on my own.

Sam Cook offered to take me to the house of death during one of my numerous visits to The Walls. We entered the funeral home via a gate that was comprised of chains. As I entered, found three tiny waiting rooms to my left. These are the places where prisoners are held for forty eight hours before being executed. A few chairs that fold and small tables with editions in the Bible in English and Spanish are found in the area between the cells. To the left is the entryway for the death cell. It's painted with the same green used in inside the internal cinderblock area. This disinfectant is available in my nose. It was as if I was in the smell of a hospital. The room was barely nine feet in size when I was in this death chamber. A table of metal with a small pillow and mattress was at the center of the space. It was around waist-high. Although it looked a lot like the gurney of a hospital, there weren't wheels. Instead, it was supported by a larger, more robust support column made of iron within the middle. The death chamber's cold, formal appearance stood out in stark opposition to the white, cotton sheets and pillowcases which covered the mattress and pillow. Five leather straps stretched from the top of mattress to the foot. They resembled belts. Two straps were also attached to arm rests padded with padding which extended from the top of each gurney, on both the right and left side. A small set of wooden steps was also made available to prisoners to climb on the gurney. The steps were also painted in the same green of the institution. Three windows gave perspectives of the execution chamber from three rooms. The window on left of the room shows the location where Pentobarbital will be administered by officials of the state. Two rooms are available in the center. The first room is designated for relatives of the victim. While the second one is reserved for inmates members of the family.

Following the execution of the death penalty both windows are encased with curtains.

It was shocking to witness that the execution chamber was in use, no matter how one is feeling about the death penalty. The death chamber was frequently used during my period in Huntsville. On June 22, 2000, a thirty-eight-year-old African-American named Gary Graham was put to death in that room at 8:49 p.m. for the 1981 murder of Bobby Lambert. Graham was just 18 at the time and was in the midst of a 10-day criminal rampage. The charges against him comprised numerous attempted and armed murders, along with numerous assaults and an alleged brutal rape. The woman who whom he tortured, raped and abused managed to hold the gun back and was eventually arrested, he was detained and referred to the police.

Graham's case became a national spectacle. Graham was condemned to death for a total of 19 years, and had sought every legal remedy he could and even taken appeals to the U.S. Supreme Court. After his appeals were concluded, George W. Bush (the Texas Governor at the time) declined to grant an extension of his execution. He claimed that Graham was granted "...full accessibility to courts including Supreme Court. Supreme Court.

I quit a discussion with TDCJ officials at 12th Street, directly across from The Walls, later that afternoon. What I next saw was an organized chaos. The roads that surround the prison were sealed off and blocked by barricades of police. There were numerous TV news vans and reporters from all the major networks. Two hundred law enforcement personnel from Texas as well as more than 2 dozen Texas Rangers, formed a line surrounding The Walls. It was a complete chaos. Bianca Jagger and the Nation of Islam and the Nation of Islam, and members of the New Black Panther Party, protested on the northeastern part of the jail. A few protesters lit a fire to flags of the U.S. flag. Flag. A reverend Jesse Jackson was wearing a grey suit, and was walking with protesters. A large number of Black Panthers were seen walking through the streets in camouflage. They were wearing black berets as well as carrying guns. On the northwest the crowd consisted of media personnel and others protesters, including people belonging to the Ku Klux Klan. Klan members posed wearing white Klan costumes and waving Confederate war flags. It was like something out of an old Hollywood film. It all went to nothing at the final. Graham was executed and he was judged by the judgement of God as well as his victims in the tiny room at The Walls.

The normality returned the following day. It was another scorching humid, humid, June morning. Wearing white prison uniforms Prison trustees walked out of The Walls trimming hedges and collecting garbage. A lawn mower was visible in distant distance. It was like the chaos of the day before was not real like it was just a fantasy. The year would be over 39 more would be executed.

I went back the The Walls several more days later at the beginning of the morning hours, to conduct more interviews. I drove along 12th

Street towards the entrance to the building, and then parked my vehicle in a nearby parking spot. Then I saw a huge crowd of people seated on the lawn of the TDCJ building which is located across the street. The group was mainly comprised of children as well as adults. The first time I saw what I thought was an unplanned gathering, I was a bit puzzled. They sat in a corner in a waiting position for something. The northeast part of The Walls was opened by an external door that I did not even know existed. A group of 75 men suddenly moved in one line and began going west along 12th Street in my direction. They were dressed in old and unfitting street clothes which were provided by the local church. They rushed to women and children who were waiting in the grass nearby and walked off and walked away from the crowd. The men waiting in line were inmates who were released from prison, while the children and women who were waiting at the front were family members. When they looked through the crowd I could see several of the women on tiptoes and shifting their heads to the left or right. There were many tears and hugs as wives were united and their children were returned with their fathers. It was a truly amazing experience. According to legend, the family of a man goes with his to prison whenever they go.

Long lines of men forming in front of The Walls reminded of another long line. It was in a different location and at a different date. It occurred in February 1991, which was a tenth of a decade ago. I was a part of a heavily-armed military convoy that was traveling northeast on Highway 50 in northern Saudi Arabia. In the Persian Gulf War was in full in full. My unit just had left Hafar Al Batin, Saudi Arabia. We were headed to Ar Ruqi which is a tiny village located that borders Saudi Arabia. Then we would cross into Iraq before heading further into Kuwait for the purpose of intercepting Iraqi Republican Guard. The two-lane, narrow road was narrow and asphalted. The convoy spanned miles. The road was bordered by vast deserts for miles. The atmosphere was filled with terror. They were low and dark and threatening. The war seemed far away to me up until that point. But then, I realized the dangers ahead. Another convoy was heading to the south, and was moving towards the north. The convoy was comprised of hundreds on hundreds of trucks as well as automobiles of all brands and models. Every vehicle was filled mattresses, clothes and kitchen appliances. The convoy was full of Saudi's and Kuwaitis who were fleeing war zones as well as their possessions. It was my first encounter dealing with war. It was my first time as a soldier, and was performing my duties. But, I realized that war had had an immense impact on a lot more people, besides my own small mortar team. I was thinking the same when I saw the men depart The Walls that morning to hug their families.

Seventy-five percent of the more than 20000 Texas prisoners released every the year out of Texas prisons got released the same day. The former convicts, who did not have families waiting for their return, walked the two blocks from their destination at the Huntsville Greyhound Bus station on the intersection of Avenue J and 12th Street. They gave a ticket for transportation for prisoners at the counter for tickets. The couple hopped on their Greyhound shuttle bus for their Texas county and received an opportunity to relive living a better life.

It's not every day that people get out of prison. I once interviewed an inmate at the Missouri State Penitentiary [6060 Lafayette Street in Jefferson City. In the time he was serving an eight-year term for assault. I was informed that by the public defense attorney the judge had found him guilty of sexual assault on the basis of the evidence of the trial. But, he suggests that you investigate out the evidence anyway.

After passing through security and security, I was permitted to go into a tiny interviewing area. After a short time, Lamar Caruthers came in and was handcuffed. He was a tall black male. He was sentenced for sexual assault. I told Lamar the fact that I am his investigator , and the lawyer he had was an attorney who was public. It is not permitted in prison to inquire about the reason why they are being held in prison. They'll explain that they are in prison if they choose to. A lot of them tell you lies and claim they didn't commit the crime regardless of what the incident was. I knew precisely what Lamar was up to. He said he was innocent.

"I did not rape that little girl." Stormy is an African-American woman in her early thirties , who was constantly in contact along with the one who suffered. He said his explanation that Stormy was "all involved You know." Caruthers as well as many other inmates, was a dropout at the end of sixth grade. He was a poor student. English skills were not great and unprofessional. If we wanted to discover an exulpatory proof, I had to know the specifics. He stated, "We were all getting involved." "And at the point I had finished You know exactly what I'm talking about...she was telling me to"Stop!. I didn't. "So I'm done." It sounded suspicious to me, but Lamar was found guilty and is currently in jail.

Stormy was later interviewed. Stormy was tall, dark-haired, tall woman who had tattoos that depicted her Tasmanian Devil on her left side bicep. She basically told the exact story, however she stated that she began saying "stop" prior to the incident. The medical report submitted after the rape did not show any signs of tears, bruising or other signs that could be indicative of sexual assault. Stormy acknowledged that Lamar might have believed Stormy telling him "no" is part of the sexual game. Lamar was the one who was in the prison cell, as Stormy took cigarette after cigarettes.

Lamar isn't something I consider to be true. I'm not denying that Stormy was mistaken. The race factor was certainly a factor in Stormy's belief. The point I want to make is that the truth and what we think of as truth may sometimes be quite different. Don't believe all you hear in taking the word of someone else. Benjamin Franklin said that you must not trust all you hear, and only half of what you observe. Private investigators are able to listen to the opinions of each participant. Truth always lies somewhere between. I'm not talking about the concept of moderation. I recommend that everyone bring their own experience and beliefs on the scene. Understanding the individuals who were involved will be the initial step in knowing the causes and how it transpired. Lamar got released from jail at the at the end.

Bryan, Texas' minimum security federal prison camp, was an incredibly beautiful prisons that I have ever been to. FPC Bryan, as it was known by the BOP located on Ursuline Avenue. It is an idyllic, lovely area with a winding residential street and homes shaded by huge Live Oak trees. It is made up of white stucco houses and red roofs made of terracotta. This isn't Alcatraz. It's actually more of the look of a private school than an official federal prison. There are no roaming security guards , and there aren't any tall guard towers. There's no fence. A minimum-security prison can house around 900 female prisoners at the same moment. Lea Fastow (wife of Andrew Fastow) who was the former CFO of Enron was one of the guests. There were many other women who were disgraced as politicians, but not widely known outside of their respective communities. Troy Gilchrist, an associate warden once told me that all women in prison are here due to one person. Most women who were in prison were charged by the authorities with laundering money, fraud on credit cards or drug-related charges. It was because they had been associated with their boyfriends or husbands who were dealers in drugs.

In addition, I reinvestigated the federal prison officers on regular basis, I also conducted medical staff investigations such as the five gynecologists employed by the. I was summoned by the U.S. Public Health Service to College Station by the U.S. Public Health Service to conduct the Personal Subject Interview (or PRSI) for Gwen Robinson. To get an official security clearance through the government candidates have to pass the PRSI. This is a lengthy personal interview. I discovered that she had been at four Federal prisons in the past 12 years, when I looked over her SF Form 86 prior to my interview. She was been moved four times in the past 12 years. Gwen's roommate at present was Chynna Swenson. She was her roommate in all four of her prior residences. Wanda Ashworth, my supervisor was intrigued by this. The supervisor believed Gwen might be an lesbian, and that Chynna was a person of color. It wasn't a big deal. It was true that the U.S. government did have specific regulations regarding homosexuality as well as secure clearances in the past. They were still able to hold an authorization. It was not the problem. The primary concern for the government was knowing who was aware of the person's life style and if they were prone to being targeted. If it was discovered that the individual was gay and the friends and family members knew the information, then the government thought they were less likely to be extorted or perform a bribe. It was possible to exploit their lifestyle to compel the person to divulge classified information or placing their lives in danger by putting them under pressure to go to prison. However, that was not my choices. Personally, I did not care. I believed that the question of whether someone was gay, or straight , was an individual choice. It wasn't my responsibility and neither was the federal government's. But, the government had strict regulations for security clearances I was required to follow. Gwen was not able to be publicly asked if her identity was lesbian because of privacy and legal concerns. Gwen was required to reveal her life. When she spoken about it I was able inquire who knew about the incident and if it affected her chances of being manipulated or acting under pressure.

Gwen, Chynna, and I had lunch with them at their home in an area of peace and quiet, just next to Kyle Field. Kyle Field is the home of teams from the Texas A&M Aggies Football interesting. Both were nurses in Bryan's St. Joseph's Hospital. They also had the same size and weight and had similar hairstyles, which were short and blond. They could be siblings or brothers. They shared photos of one another throughout their homes. They both had photos that were taken by a professional photographer, as well as photographs of them doing outdoors during their time on vacation. I was able see their identities as lesbians. It was evident that their lives were not in the hands by the state. They stated that they were simply roommates, regardless of what I inquired. Although these are government regulations It was embarrassing to discuss the matter with them. Gwen was an Security clearance holder for several years, and was a perfect candidate for a clean criminal history. Both would not confess to being gay. I had my interview completed and then moved on. I didn't want to be considered a failure. It's enough for me to be me.

Team. They resembled each other they were both white women aged 29 years old. It was pretty clear that they were identical.

Chapter 9: Your Claim Is Refused

The second time I worked at USIS Huntsville saw me take on a heavier task and to work to very short deadlines. While the majority of my work was routine however, there were instances where you were interrupted in your routine by something odd. My personal opinion is that regardless of the profession a person may have there is a point where all routine gets routine. This is the case to Navy Seals and police personnel or Secret Service agents in protective particulars. It was during the delicate background investigation on national security when I realized this to be to be true. After interviewing so many people, it's easy to conclude that everybody is honest. The truth is revealed and then you go on onto the next. It's simple to overlook that certain people lie or at most, they lie. Doris Kerns Goodwin, historian claimed that the past is not only the past. It's a lens by which the subject's self-image changes filters. I found out that not every person is qualified for security clearances, contrary to what I was told by others. Frank Hamilton was included in the group.

Frank is a former student at Blinn College in Bryan, Texas. He was six feet tall, was handsome with nice looks and plenty of charm. Everybody loved Frank. He was set to be awarded the degree of an associate in crime. He also had applied for a position as an officer of the Uniformed Division of Secret Service in Washington, D.C. Frank's interview went well, as I remember. To learn more about the process, I kept in touch using both the researched and sourced sources. Frank was a fierce racist.

Frank's background check revealed that Lola an individual I spoke with, was with Frank for the majority of in his life, if he even existed. We had a meeting in Burger Boy in Bryan, close to Blinn College. Lola was medium-sized with straight long, straight blonde hair that fell down to her shoulders. The outfit she was sporting were faded Levi's Blue jeans and a black short-sleeve Burger Boy Polo shirt. The moment I arrived she was completed her shift. We walked across the checkered blue and white floor and we slid into a corner booth away from the ear of all. I handed over my credentials, and took from my USIS flip notebook. I began asking the same questions I have previously asked thousands of times. Lola appeared exhausted after having worked for eight hours. Although it was close to the end of my working day I had 45 minutes before I could drive to home from Huntsville. When I finished an interview with her, I asked whether Frank's actions could make him ineligible as a security guard. After a short time she came out in what could be an instant of clarity. This immediately woke me up from my brain fog that I had induced by routine.

"Excuse us?" She was required to define the meaning of what Frank was referring to when she stated that Frank was a racist.

She hesitated. She hesitated. She told him that she was a nigger while she was with him. He was a nipper I believe. His buddies made fun of the black community and made black jokes. They discussed their desire to take out African-Americans, and then join KKK.

Interesting. It was particularly fascinating, since I'd talked to a few of these supposed friends , and none ever mentioned this particular incident. Frank wanted to become an Washington, D.C. police officer, one of the cities with more than fifty percent of African-Americans.

"And do you feel, Lola?" "Is this something you are happy with?" I asked?

She responded, "Ofcourse not." She started to feel somewhat disoriented. That was actually the reason we parted. He constantly tells me that I'm different and it became too for me. It seemed like initially a joke. I quickly realized that the man was serious.

Though it was the fault of an ex-girlfriend, it was a serious charge. It was real, regrettably. Lola provided me with the names of sources who confirmed her claim. Frank Hamilton was denied security clearance and was not able to accept a position in the Uniformed Division in Washington, D.C. Frank wasn't the only candidate for government positions I could find. Paul had also been involved.

Paul Benavidez, the youngest of four children was the son of a rancher from Alpine Texas. He was a candidate for a position for the U.S. Border Patrol. I drove to the city in the west of Texas in order to do a background check.

Alpine A small town that is home to six thousand residents to the north from Big Bend National Park is the county seat of Brewster County. The year 1956 saw the creation of the Warner County seat. Warner

Brothers production Giant was shot in the vicinity of. The hotel is also home to Sul Ross University, where Paul graduated with a degree in sociology. It is also home to the Holland Hotel. Holland Hotel is a Texas Historic Landmark which was constructed in 1912. It is located in the area of West Holland Avenue, in the downtown area of Alpine. It is located in Alpine, on West Holland Avenue. Century Grill is located within the hotel and offers the most delicious steak you'll ever have the pleasure of tasting. Do not demand steak sauce. You won't be resentful by the chef. It's not needed. It's so delicious, you'll be tempted to hit your grandmother.

Paul also had an older brother named Earnest whom I found to be nothing but uninteresting. When I was conducting Paul's background research I discovered Earnest's ex-wife Sylvia. Sylvia was a resident of an older mobile house damaged, and had several vehicles in various states of disrepair located near Marfa Texas, which is approximately 30 minutes to the west of Alpine. Sylvia said to me that Earnest as well as Paul are Coyotajes. She told me that they operated a business of their own transporting illegal immigrants across the TexasMexican frontier for a small fee. Paul's main goal was for him to be hired by the border guard. This will help them make their task of smuggling much easier and also more lucrative.

At first, I did not believe in her story. I'd like to see more evidence, similar to the allegations made by Lola regarding Frank Hamilton. The usual practice is for the government to not speak to an ex-partner because they're not able to provide any evidence that is positive. When I continued to speak with others, a more complete picture was revealed. It was evident that the Benavidez brothers also had a side business that involved trafficking. Paul was not granted an official security clearance from Border Patrol officials from the U.S. Border Patrol and was refused an invitation to be a part of their team.

In my time in Huntsville I frequented the INS in the Inn [67] located on the south-facing side. It was a basic and unassuming structure with only one story that was located off the state highway 75. There were deportation agents working within the offices. They were charged with expatriating non-U.S. citizens from the TDCJ and its surrounding regions. They conducted frequent meetings, regular reinvestigations and plenty of time spent in the TDCJ.

Robert Macklemore, one the many deportation officers , began inquire about my security clearance. He was athletic and small and had worked in the INS for over 10 years. I didn't really think much about his concerns. I was aware that the regular renewal was nearing and I thought he would want to be prepared for what was to come. It was five years since the last time he had a reinvestigation. Perhaps the procedure has changed. It was strange that he hadn't had to go through the procedure twice before. In the end, I learned that OPM had an immense case backlog. This is why there was no guarantee that all government employees were being reinvestigated every five years in the manner that is required. I then forget about it and ignored it. It was all fine with regards to his PRSI. I don't remember any issues. He was honest and transparent.

Then, a few months later, I was back. After returning at the exact INS office to conduct further interviews, it became apparent on me that Robert was absent during the past few months. He was pleasant and made it a habit to greet me every day. Perhaps he moved. I tried to talk to one of the deportation officers, but he stared at me in a blank way. He said, sheepishly, "No." I was struck by the manner in which he responded "No" and then I realized that the truth of the story. I visited Cindy Hayes' office, who was the supervisory agent. She is also my contact person. After a bit of gentle prodding she told the whole amazing story to me.

Robert who was originally from Falfurrias in Texas He was away for a couple of weeks. In the Border Patrol station south Falfurrias stopped the red 1999 Ford Escort driving north on Highway 281. Three Mexicans tried to illegally be admitted to this U.S. from Mexico, the three people in the vehicle turned out into their. This isn't atypical. It happens every day. It was interesting to find it was the case that Ford Escort was registered to Robert Macklemore when the Border Patrol examined the plates. After further inspections, they realized the fact that Robert Macklemore was an Macklemore was also a Macklemore, who was recently completing his routine review. Robert also had a second business, it was discovered. Robert was the straight-laced INS officer in charge of enforcing laws governing the United States' immigration laws. He used his expertise and position to aid illegal immigration. He wasn't aware of what it would cost the person.

employees for government employees of U.S. government. Robert

INS Deportation Officer. Yes it was Robert

Robert wasn't the sole government worker who took advantage of Robert. It was what I learned when I started to investigate Bobby "Skip" as an agent of Special Agent Pilots for Drug Enforcement.

Administration (DEA). Skip was a surveillance officer and provided air support to DEA operations in intelligence and the drug enforcement operations located in Houston, Texas. I was surprised when Skip didn't return my numerous phone calls. Then I went into In the Woods Aviation Service located in Montgomery County north of Houston and discovered the hanger that is secretly used by the DEA. It was a basic building that was situated at a tiny airport, surrounded by dense pine trees that are found in East Texas. Becker's supervisor wasn't adamant initially but eventually he was willing to talk with me. After realizing that I was not going to disappear, he acknowledged that Skip disappeared. He also was able to have hundreds of thousands of drug money that was recently seized. Interviews were not conducted. Although I'm not certain whether Skip was ever arrested by the DEA However, it is known that BLM, the Bureau of Land Management (BLM) eventually got Eleanor. Because I spotted her, I'm sure.

Eleanor Swift was a hazel eyed brunette with shoulder-length eyes. She weighed about 200 pounds and was about five foot tall. The federal agency that is responsible for the management of public areas within Oklahoma is her boss, which was the BLM. Eleanor suffered a back injury at workand submitted a workers' compensation claim. She fell in the term used to describe"a "slip-and-fall" within the field. She was thrown off the roof. At work. Based on her medical doctor she was unable to walk or stand for long durations of time. She was not able to move over 10lbs. Eleanor did not leave home, being advised she not put her feet on the ground. When the weeks turned to days and weeks turned into the months Eleanor started to doubt whether she was trying to hide malingering. [68]

Eleanor as well as the majority of people who commit compensation fraud, started working in secret at a different job that doubled her earnings. Eleanor will pay a high cost for her fraudulent acts in the eyes of authorities in the US government.

Eleanor was an Oklahoman resident living in a town in rural Oklahoma town. It was later discovered that Eleanor was fine. Her health was good, aside of the fact she was paid bi-weekly for workers' compensation as well as a payment for her salary. Eleanor took the decision to go after her idea of opening her own restaurant while at home getting workers' compensation. This is what Eleanor did. In the moment I was employed in USIS Dallas and was asked to look into Eleanor. To discover details about Eleanor I got my trusted surveillance vehicle and drove north on Oklahoma's state road 69.

Surveillance may not be what you think it will be. It may take several days to complete and can be inconvenient. It is the nature of surveillance. Eleanor was an exception. I was driving to Atoka, Oklahoma when I observed Eleanor going out of her eatery, "Eleanor's Home Cooking." This was so terrible she was unable to move more than 10 pounds or stand or walk for prolonged periods and couldn't even carry a crate full of tomatoes.

She was back at home at the time I turned around to retrace our steps, before returning to her. I swiftly installed security cameras at her restaurant. She got in the silver Ford F350 pickup truck and left the restaurant after 30 minutes. She was only five feet tall, and had to struggle to get into the cabin. I recorded the incident on film, and then I followed her to a self-service car wash. I observed her scrub, brush and wash her car for about 30 minutes. This was a lot more than what she claimed she did for her injuries. My car drove her to home at night after which she made a decision to go back to my hotel to get a new beginning.

The next day I had an excellent morning breakfast in Bledsoe's Diner before heading through the Atoka County Courthouse. To prove the small-scale enterprise, I obtained copies of her business license and the DBA in the Atoka County Courthouse. After that, I visited The Atoka County Times. It's the local newspaper. I wrote news stories about Eleanor's opening ceremony. One of the stories featured a heartfelt personal piece on Eleanor's struggle to achieve her desire to open the restaurant. The front cover featured an image of Eleanor smiling while holding a pair huge scissors as she prepared for the ceremony of cutting the ribbon and the big opening celebration of Atoka County Chamber of Commerce.

It was time for lunch after all that long hours of work. I felt the need to prepare my meal at home and knew precisely where to find it. Then I returned my vehicle, and drove toward Eleanor's Restaurant. There was a rumble on the wooden floor when I arrived at the restaurant. I sat in an open area in front of a table that was covered in blue cloth. This allowed me to see at the cooking area. It was absolutely beautiful. It was rustic and had a log cabin feel like Cracker Barrel. It served comfort food in an intimate restaurant.

Eleanor arrived at my table shortly thereafter with a pencil and notepad. Even though we exchanged pleasantries but she was unsure of who I was, nor the reason for my presence. I asked her a number of questions before she signed my request. Then, I got her responses documented on my document. It appeared as if I was asking her questions casually. It was really a claim. She was unaware of that she was making a statement. I verified that she had been the proprietor of the restaurant and that it was operating since the beginning of March. I confirmed that she was working between ten and 12 hours per day, seven days a week, and with very little time for rest. She stated that she was much of her time in the gym. She said she served as proprietor as well as the cook in charge and an waitress. She also was a fraudster of federal funds. It is true the fact that she had a solid character.

After returning to Dallas I sent my video and report. Initial feedback on my investigation wasn't given. A few months after I received a commendation note to the BLM regional director where Eleanor was working. I found out that she was accused of fraud, and eventually, she was transferred to federal jail. Friedrich Nietzsche, a German philosopher, once wrote that "The lies are a fact in our lives." It's an idea Eleanor Swift would understand and ultimately pay for.

Although Eleanor's deed was terrible however, it paled in comparison to Vincent Lewiston. For something that occurred 10 years ago, Vincent would have lost his security certificate. Vincent was thin and tall and had long black curls and blue eyes that could see right through your eyes. Vincent was employed by Idaho National Laboratory, the U.S. defense contractor Idaho National Laboratory west Idaho Falls located in the south-east of Idaho. Vincent was a Q clearance holder at the DOE. He worked at the labs for almost two decades. Rita Vincent's ex-wife was interviewed on one of his frequent reconsultations. Rita said that Vincent had the girls sexually assaulted 10 years ago.

Ex-spouses' statements like I have mentioned previously generally are considered with a grain of salt. The government often won't allow to speak with an ex-wife, or husband. They're rarely able give a fair and impartial perspective on the matter. Vincent And Rita divorce was bitter. Rita is well-known as alcohol-dependent. She drank Peach Schonapps, her favorite adult drink. Another reason why Rita's comments did not receive the respect they merited was that Rita appeared to be untrustworthy.

Vincent and Rita's tale was quite like that of John A. Walker Jr. Walker was a U.S. Navy Chief Warrior Officer who gave classified documents to KGB from 1968 until retire in 1983. Walker took classified information and operated with impunity for fifteen years. Barbara Crowley, Walker's ex-wife knew about his spying activities, however she was also a alcoholic who was not first questioned due to the reasons I mentioned. In the end, however, the FBI at first dismissed her as being a drunk after they finally questioned her. She said she was angry with her husband and was willing to try anything to hurt his career.

Rita did not appear in Vincent's earlier periodic revisits. However, she was identified as a possible interviewer this time. The government finally determined to look into her claims and confirm her claim. It makes sense to start with her daughters. Tiffany was my youngest daughter was my interviewee.

Tiffany Lewiston was nineteen years old when she enrolled at in the University of Texas at Arlington. She was on campus with me and we went to the soundproofed study room located on the third floor within the Central Library. Her brunette-looking hair is pulled in by her, and she put it into the ponytail. It was hard to tell she was sad. A bright pink hoodie was sported by her, along with worn Blue Levi's jeans. She also carried a navy blue backpack. Tiffany seemed like the college student.

The first rule is preparation when interviewing. I was well-versed in the investigation from beginning to the end. Like Gwen Robinson's background inquiry in FPC Bryan, I was obliged to adhere to certain privacy restrictions and legal requirements. Vincent had the right to certain rights. The abuse was just an assertion. It was impossible to inquire of Tiffany "Did your father sexually assault me?" Vincent was a veteran with a successful career, with an impeccable track record. It was a challenge for me to persuade Tiffany to confess to sexual abuse in the event that it had occurred. In order to make this happen I first had to establish trust.

We discussed her education while I interviewed her. We also talked about Texas. We also discussed her part-time position in the field of dental assistance in the nearby dental clinic. Although it was at first difficult but I soon discovered a common ground with her. I began to mimic her body speech.

Communication is mostly non-verbal. Mirroring is a method to build trust and rapport in your relationship with the person you are talking to. Mirroring can be used to mimic your subject's movements and patterns of speech. It is a way to start sounding and move in the same way as the subject. You'll start to look and sound like them. You will be able to copy their hand expressions, facial expressions, and sitting position and mimic their language. It's not apparent. It's more subtle than the other. Tiffany was raised in a town in the countryside. She was slower to speak and more thoughtful than people from cities. They are more likely to speak more quickly and more clearly, and also will have more things to share. Once I was able to establish the rapport, I was hesitant to ask tough questions.

Interviews on sexual abuse are like every other interview. They require specifics. It's not enough just to claim that the person was a mole or touched you. Different people are different in their interpretations. An investigator needs to gather specific information to identify the nature and severity of the violence. This will help them determine what really occurred. The obvious issues are, such as what, when when, and at what frequency. It was a challenge for me to persuade Tiffany whom I had only seen just 20 minutes prior to open up about these dark painful and difficult memories. Tiffany had spent years trying to forget these painful memories.

It was discovered Vincent's wife Rita proved right. She could have been drunk. However, she was probably right regarding Vincent. The government was unable to take action. Tiffany experienced a hard in understanding the father-daughter bond. I began to speak to Tiffany and she said, "I want to let you know that I talked to your mom." Then , I added a psychological gap and let my words to linger in the air and awaiting acknowledgment. Tiffany was believed to be telling the truth she had divulged all of her secrets to me, and I informed her. At the end of the day I persuaded Tiffany to come forward and provide me with the details. It all began in the presence of her younger sister Sherry. Tiffany was first aware of this as her dad would come into the bedroom in the evening and take Sherry by the hand and then leave the room.

Vincent began sexually assaulting Sherry at the age of 16 years old. Sherry was able to resist Vincent's efforts to make her feel better. She was 13 at the time of the incident and it went on for 2 years. Tiffany could not recall specific dates. The incident occurred about once a week Tiffany said. He did not have sexual relations with her , but more often sex on her breasts and her female genitals. He would make her do oral sex and she would perform the same thing for him. Tiffany was interested in knowing about the time and date the session was over. She was unable to pinpoint exactly when it came to an end. There were a lot of memories from the time however they were blurred. It was as if she was lost in the middle of a fog. It was not her fault. It's a terrible experience that no one would like to be remembered.

It appeared that she believed her mother was returning late in the evening from a bar and then came up to them. Rita in her drunken state, threatened Vincent. She claimed that should Vincent had touched their daughters in the future she would shoot the man first before calling the police. She also made comments saying that she could take out an individual body part with the rusty scissors. He was able to understand the message. Her father got up to work the following morning while Tiffany and Sherry returned to school. Sherry's mother never mentioned the incident ever again. It was as if there was no incident. Tiffany was often apprehensive about her mother's return as well as the image of her father walking into Tiffany was an illusion. In just 6 months of her birth, the father had gone and Rita became divorced. Tiffany as well as Sherry were the only ones to be able to communicate with their father.

Tiffany dropped her head and gazed down at the earth. She cried softly as her eyes flooded with tears. Each word came out clearly precisely pronounced. In the quiet of her soundproof study her words appeared to hang. She couldn't discern the details of that horrible dream, however it was hanging above her like clouds. She pulled out her hoodie, put the hood on top of her head, and attempted to cover up the awful events from so many years ago. It was my desire to soothe her and tell her everything would be okay. It would have been insensitive. It was difficult to witness her suffer, and to realize her to be the person to open her wounds, and that nobody could have comforted her.

With mixed feelings I made my way across campus to get to my car following the interview. I felt relieved and happy that Tiffany had been honest. I had accomplished my mission. However, I was embarrassed of having to remind her of the sexual assault and make it difficult for her to go back to the painful memories. She'd spent the majority time trying to erase the hurt. However, I needed to locate her father. After listening to her story I was convinced by her. He was going to lose his security clearance and he wouldn't work for the DOE. Idaho also did not have a law of limitations on sexual assaults on children under sixteen years of age. Vincent's life eventually caught up with Vincent after 10 years. The only problem was that he was not aware of it. Tiffany Lewiston interviewed me and it was a hit. The interview was a expensive cost.

Chapter 10: Citizen 4 And The Promises Of Usis

Patriot Day. Every American knows precisely where they are, and exactly what happened on September 11th 2001. The day began for me as well as many others, as any other day. The moments of the day will remain forever in our memories. It was a bright and cool autumn morning. A customer walked up to me from the U.S. Post Office Huntsville, Texas and stated that an airplane struck the World Trade Center in New York City. I initially believed it was a small , private plane that crashed into one of the towers. While it appeared unlikely, I thought the pilot was sick or lost the ability to follow. I drove to my car and switched the radio off. It was 9:03 AM. While I was listening to live news updates from United Airlines Flight 175 colliding into the South Tower of the World Trade Center I was sitting down with the door to the driver's compartment open. The incident was a tragic accident. Two planes crashing into the World Trade Center was a rare event. America was in danger.

I had already scheduled interviews with teachers from New Waverly High School, just off the 75 state highway located in New Waverly. After hearing the first news report on my car radio , I was uncertain about what to do. I was not fully aware of the magnitude of the incident at this point , so I continued working as usual. Thirty minutes later, reached the school to discover it locked down. I was only a few minutes' drive between Huntsville towards New Waverly when American Airlines Flight 77 crashed into the Pentagon which killed the 49 passengers on board. The Pentagon also killed more than a hundred twenty-five civilians as well as military.

Before I was allowed to get in, I was required show him my government papers. Students and staff were huddled in the same area. The attack was unique. This attack was unheard of. This was the most severe attack on the U.S. homeland has not been attacked as viciously ever since Pearl Harbor. We were all shocked and did not think of what we could do. As we made our way to his workplace, the chief was carrying a radio with two channels in his hand. I turned to him and told me, "You chose a bad day to interview."

It was prior to the advent of smartphones as well as social media, and their widespread nature of.

The internet. The majority of the information was available through radio and television. It was difficult for me to concentrate on my work day as I listened at the radio inside my vehicle. It was difficult to obtain details from individuals, have normal conversations, and gather public information. My experiences were not even close to other areas of the country. Wanda was my Dallas manager was the one who had the previous day to continue doing the same job as usual. To be fair, Wanda was advising us to work just as normal. It was before the terrorist attacks began and we were able to comprehend the severity of the incident. In the afternoon I realized how futile and drove my car back towards home. After returning to my house that evening, I was watching news on the television. I still recall looking at the television in my living room. I was shocked.

My job was impacted by the events of 9/11. It took me several weeks me to recuperate of the trauma. The following areas affected areas were affected: Schools, shops, banks and airports were all had to be shut down for a time. We didn't know if there would be another round of attacks since the attack took place on Tuesday. In the following week, I received an email from USIS. I was advised to try my best, but be aware of the emotions of other people. Even after a few weeks it was difficult to sit down and talk to individuals. These events were deeply felt by all.

The 11th September of the year gave way to a very sad Christmas season. It was a time of sadness for the entire world. World Trade Center fires continued to burn throughout December, providing constant reminders of the fact that we were under attack. Smoke could be seen far away or from space. The situation slowly returned to normal by the start of 2002. Osama bin Laden who was the leader al-

Qaeda's Islamic terrorist group , and the main culprit behind the terrorist attack of 9/11 was not killed for another 10 years. In May of 2011 Bin Laden was snatched up on the third level of the basement of his Abbottabad, Pakistan home. Bin Laden was beaten to death by the Chief Petty officer Senior Robert J. O'Neill, Seal Team 6. Then, he hit the radio button and said "For God, country...Geronimo Geronimo Geronimo."

In the beginning of the year I was able to go on an investigation report out of Ft. Worth to collect statements from Lockheed employees.

Martin plant. After having an interview with one of the employees the plant asked me if would like to visit.

The F-16 fighter plane was built at the plant at the time of production. The warehouse was that production was conducted. It was the place where production took place. F-16 was a tiny piece of steel that could be held in your hands during the start of the production line. It took on the look of a fighter plane as it went as it progressed through manufacturing. While this plane was being offered to U.S. allies, I asked him if he'd encountered any issues. He smiled and said, "Well, we have the Saudi's and Israeli's to prevent them from encountering each other during they visit."

I also was in Clear Lake, south of Houston at NASA's Johnson Space Center. I was able to conduct a variety of background investigations regarding the security of the nation's NASA engineers who were involved in the development of the robotic arm of the spacecraft. Although the arm was developed by an Canadian business, NASA had its own engineers working on the project at JSC. I expected that the NASA offices to appear modern and futuristic, like something from Star Wars. They were like every other office in the government regardless of the fact that they were established in the year 1960. It had a variety of cubicles, computers desks and dry erase board. It was difficult to pass the entrances of NASA, particularly given that many of my interview were scheduled to be private. The procedure was to be astonished and not allow the interviewee to speak about the visit or write an explanation. A federal identification badge along with ID were enough to allow me through the entryway. Like my Lockheed-Martin tour I was offered the same excursion at JSC.

The U.S. Bureau of Engraving and Printing's west currency facility located in Ft. Worth was probably the most interesting and secure facility I've ever visited. Although it was on Blue Mound Road, finding the entrance for public use was difficult. It seemed as if they wanted to prevent people from entering. It is only possible to be admitted to the facility if anticipate someone. This made visits by surprise to the facility a lot more challenging. It took around 30 minutes to reach an individual on the line and describe the reason I was there. I then drove to a different security gate where federal security guards utilized a mirror to check of my vehicle. They employed dogs to look under my vehicle for explosives. It was also requested to unzip my trunk and hood so they could look inside. Be aware my U.S. government credentials. When I reached the location, I needed to go through another security gate. I was required empty my pockets before handing over my mobile. Also, the magnetometer was required. The employee offered to help me, and I settled down on a comfy couch in the lobby, while waiting. It took me the whole morning to finish the whole procedure, and the entire interview.

After my interview, an person who was interviewing me led me on a suspended walkway with glass, which allowed people to view beneath the floors. It was the backstage experience. I've never witnessed this much money in my life. The floor was filled with piles of cash wooden pallets, filled with $100 bills and other things. My guide stated that money can make people insane. When I left the building and returned to my car at the end of afternoon, his words stayed in my mind. It was most likely time to shift shifts. Parking lots were packed with workers carrying huge transparent plastic bags which contained their lunch and wallets inside. Another security measure to ensure that the money isn't stolen.

There's always the possibility of. The year 2006 was the time a federal employees, David Faison, would be able to steal $67,000.00 worth of unfinished, one hundred dollar bills. The bills were thrown into casinos in New Jersey, Delaware, and West Virginia by Faison, who then exchanged them for legitimate bills. When casino managers noticed that the bills weren't serialized or bore been sealed with the U.S. Treasury seal, Faison was finally found guilty.

My investigation would lead me to other issues. A number of them were involved in issues with drugs or alcohol-related abuse cases, civil suits, and other forms of arrests. A prime example was the mystery of Melissa Sloan, the disappearing lawyer. It turned out to not be a major mystery in the end.

The appointment I had was set for Monday morning in Melissa's Downtown Houston office. Melissa was a lawyer in the government in the U.S. Department of Labor. She was due for routine reconsultation. Everything had gone as planned up to the point at which. To remind her of the appointment I left her a message on my voicemail late on Sunday evening. I did not hear from her. On Monday I drove to her office at S. Gessner Drive. From there I took a peaceful elevator until the eleventh floor. After what seemed to be to be a long time her secretary walked slowly across the room with a sad look in her eyes. "I'm regretful," the secretary said however "we are unable to find her." She's not been at work today and hasn't answered any of her phone calls.

I went back to work. I tried calling her and write her during the entire day. I never received a reply. It was as if she had disappeared. I was under a lot of pressure to deliver results in schedule for my customer. I had to do my due diligence. I called her a few more times before I was capable of locating her in just five minutes. It was amazing to be able to meet her.

Melissa Sloan was my inspiration. I took note of this suggestion and will be able to recall it in the near future. The girl wasn't abducted or captured by an organized crime group. And she didn't forget about the conversation. She was away from at home. She wasn't working or in the court. She was not even dead. Melissa Sloan was the government attorney for DOL and was in prison. In the evening of Sunday, she was charged for driving being under the influence Houston's best. She was at the time in downtown jail as guests. Because of her shame and embarrassed, she did not call anyone. This is in addition to the reality that the consequences of a DUI arrest could be a catastrophe to her security clearance.

The negative consequences like the DUI by an attorney are called issues from the federal government. Each period, USIS evaluated my performance and determined that the percentage of problems I initiated on my subjects was only one of many numbers. My percentage was consistently greater than the standard. They always desired more. Unexpectedly, it was this factor that would cause the end of a fantastic firm. The problem was that no one knew about that when it happened.

My work with USIS advanced and I eventually was able to conduct background security investigations for a different client that was which was the National Reconnaissance Office (or NRO) an obscure intelligence organization of the U.S. government. The NRO was charged with constructing and operating secret surveillance satellites. These spy satellites, which are classified, are used by the federal government to collect information on enemies and friendly governments. Its identity NRO as well as the precise name of the company were secret until the end of September in 1992.

The NRO subjects were among the top. Their only complaint was the speeding ticket. The work was highly separated. To store the files I was given an additional laptop protected by various layers of encryption and password security. I took a flight from Fairfax in Virginia to receive instruction in a plain building that was located within an office space 15 miles away distant from the Pentagon. It was a quiet place. NRO investigative process was classified. USIS personnel were referred to the investigation under the name of Air Force investigations (or the Air Force contract) to ensure the operational security. While he wasn't named or wore a uniform with a the name on it I was trained by him to fulfill the contract.

The year passed by as the demands to produce the results required by USIS increased. It was not uncommon to travel more than 100 miles in a day and work as many as ten hours per day in the final year of my work with USIS. This was six days a week. The advantage of being able to work this way was that it meant I earned good money from all of my working overtime. But I didn't have enough time or the energy to invest the money. Huntsville was sometimes referred to as"a "one-person job post" however I needed to manage the investigative work of at least two people. The reality that USIS appointed two full-time investigators shortly after I quit the company is more an indication of the.

The frantic work schedule was not just experienced in Huntsville. It was felt throughout the entire company. USIS is responsible for about 60% of all U.S. government background investigation and was paid around 200 million dollars annually in compensation. CACI, Keypoint, and MSM Security Services all fought to get a larger piece of the pie that the government eats. Investigators are likely to make concessions to meet their objectives if working under stress or pressure to meet deadlines. This was exactly the case. It could be that the company was ambitious and expanded too quickly. USIS was eventually an unfortunate victim of the company's own successes. At the end of 2001, I was able to quit USIS. It was long before problems began to become grave. The investigation started by a whistleblower, which resulted in investigation by the Internal Department of Justice investigation. Two incidents that appeared to be unrelated made the matter more complicated. These two incidents, both of which were both just four months after each other, were able to attract the attention of an U.S. official. This ultimately led to USIS being unable to renew their OPM contract.

In the beginning the notorious National Security Agency contractor (NSA) who was codenamed Citizen Four, was involved. It happened in May 2013 during the time that Edward Snowden, a Booz Allen Hamilton contractor, was on time off from his work as an analyst for systems with the NSA.

Snowden was seen leaving the tunnel, which was a secret NSA facility located in Hawaii in Hawaii, where he worked on an aircraft that contained classified information that was stolen. His supervisor informed him that it was time to return to the U.S. for medical treatment. However, he didn't show up. In the end, he flew to Moscow and then on to Hong Kong.

Edward Snowden was born in Elizabeth City (North Carolina) on June 21, 1983.

Carolina through Lonnie Snowden, and Elizabeth Snowden. He was a member of the

U.S. Army Reserve, and enrolled in Special Forces Training to become a Green Beret. After suffering leg injuries in training, he was dismissed after just four months. He was a part of the CIA in the year following and became a specialist in computer security. Then, in the year 2009, he left the CIA and started working for Dell Computer. He was later contracted out to NSA and was eventually transferred to its Ft. Meade facility. He began to steal classified documents from NSA prior to his transfer in 2012 to the Hawaii Regional Operations Center. This is also in which he was found to be violating the 17th Amendment to Espionage Act. Booz Allen Hamilton was the last consulting position before he handed the thousands of documents classified to and other information for Glenn Greenwald, a journalist for The Guardian, and Laura Poitras as documentary film maker.

Snowden said he revealed secret information due to the fact that he did not wish to be a part of a system in which citizens were monitored similar to the NSA. Oliver Stone, a veteran Academy Award winner, would portray Snowden in his film Snowden as an anonymous whistleblower who was later made an icon.

Stone didn't understand the role or purpose of the NSA and created Snowden appear as Jason Bourne. In reality, he was a contractor at a lower level. Stone's portrayal of him was unbalanced.

A few months later, the next event was held. Aaron Alexis, a U.S. Navy veteran and civilian contractor has arrived on the Washington Navy Yard, Washington, D.C. on September 16th 13th, 2013. He was at the site to help in the construction of Anacostia River Bridge. The bridge was being constructed by an inter-service Navy Marine Corps computer network that was designed to aid The Experts, a private government contractor for information technology. Alexis arrived at the building 197 with a relaxed manner after passing through security. The bathroom on the fourth floor was where the man carefully put together the Remington tactical shotgun with a 12-gauge capacity in his palm. He then left and unintentionally walked around between the floors and rooms, killing twelve people while wounded three others. It was the Beretta 9mm semiautomatic pistol that he was carrying was taken away by a security guard whom he fatally shot. Following a brief gunfight Alexis was struck into the skull at the time by Dorian DeSantis, a Washington, D.C. police officer.

It was discovered the fact that Alexis had a mental disorder. He had been hearing voices. It was believed that he is controlled by high frequency electrical waves. In more than one instance the patient was treated for insomnia that was severe.

The interesting thing to observe it was the case that Snowden and Alexis were subject to security clearances investigated by the same company, USIS. This isn't atypical. USIS was responsible for the majority of security clearances issued by the government. To be truthful, USIS is not responsible for security clearances. Two cases of high profile occurred in the space of four months another, and lawmakers were able to talk about the matter and look for another person to blame.

USIS didn't know and would not have known that OPM's Inspector General as well as the DOJ started investigating the internal affairs of the company's operations in July. After being dismissed on the spot, Blake Percival, USIS director of field services filed a qui-tam [72] whistleblower lawsuit against the company. Percival's suit declared that Percival was fired for having was not able to adhere to a policy called dumped. Dumping or flushing background investigations, as used in investigator terms, is to categorize the investigations as complete even though they aren't. Percival's suit, Snowden's , and Alexis the actions of all add up to create an uproar against the company.

Following the investigation by the government It was found out that a variety of USIS employees and managers at the middle level had falsified background checks to meet deadlines. Missouri Senator Claire McCaskill said that "From Edward Snowden, to Aaron Alexis...what's becoming apparent is a pattern of failure on the part of this organization." ..."." It was a bit exaggerated given the outstanding work performed by USIS professional investigators. McCaskill evidently was in front of cameras. However, Percival's whistleblower suit and DOJ inquiry were both serious allegations. USIS was eventually accused of being sued by the U.S. government for 665,000 not satisfactory background checks. Altegrity is the company that was parent to USIS and was required to declare bankruptcy in the year 2015. All of the 2,500 support employees along with background researchers were dismissed. Although there was a lot of attention paid to USIS's actions, the bankruptcy inside would be the final nail in USIS the coffin. Alexis and Snowden initiated an investigation, which led to the consequent

My first encounter with USIS was extremely positive. Phil Harper, the CEO was always there to answer my questions and hand me an enormous amount of M&Ms from his office. They were stored in a clear glass dish which he placed at his desk. Harper was an open-door type of person. I was a rookie investigationist in the cave and Harper was helping me learn. Harper was willing to discuss what the future held for USIS any person. Harper was an ex-U.S. Army Airborne Infantry officer, and he was killed many years before USIS moved to the south.

Wanda the district supervisor, I worked with was just like Harper. She was a professional of the highest caliber. The people at USIS I worked with were excellent. A lot of the issues that affected USIS came up shortly after I quit. The company was purchased by a variety of investors. I was the sole investigator at only one duty station, a cog on the massive wheel. When I was required to meet deadlines that were impossible and deadlines, I was stressed and exhausted. I was looking for my own private investigation firm. This was the main reason for me to leave USIS.

Conclusion

There is plenty of information to sift through however, you must decide what kind of detective you'd like to become. There are a variety of different fields you can choose from, some of which are more hazardous than others, however all one is fulfilling in their own way. All it comes down to taking a look inside and knowing you are in the best position to select the appropriate best one for you. Private investigation careers is a long-term commitment, but you be able to work with a variety of people. And in the case in bounty-hunting, you are able to visit different locations. This also means that you're an upright citizen. In the end, you'd like to become an investigator in order to help others, do you not?

Do you enjoy watching the police show to find out if can answer the question ahead of them? Do you enjoy reading mystery novels and then smile when you discover you're on the right track? Are you thinking about what you could do to conduct have approached an investigation be different?

www.ingramcontent.com/pod-product-compliance
Lightning Source LLC
Chambersburg PA
CBHW050024130526
44590CB00042B/1878